THIS BOOK
IS FOR:

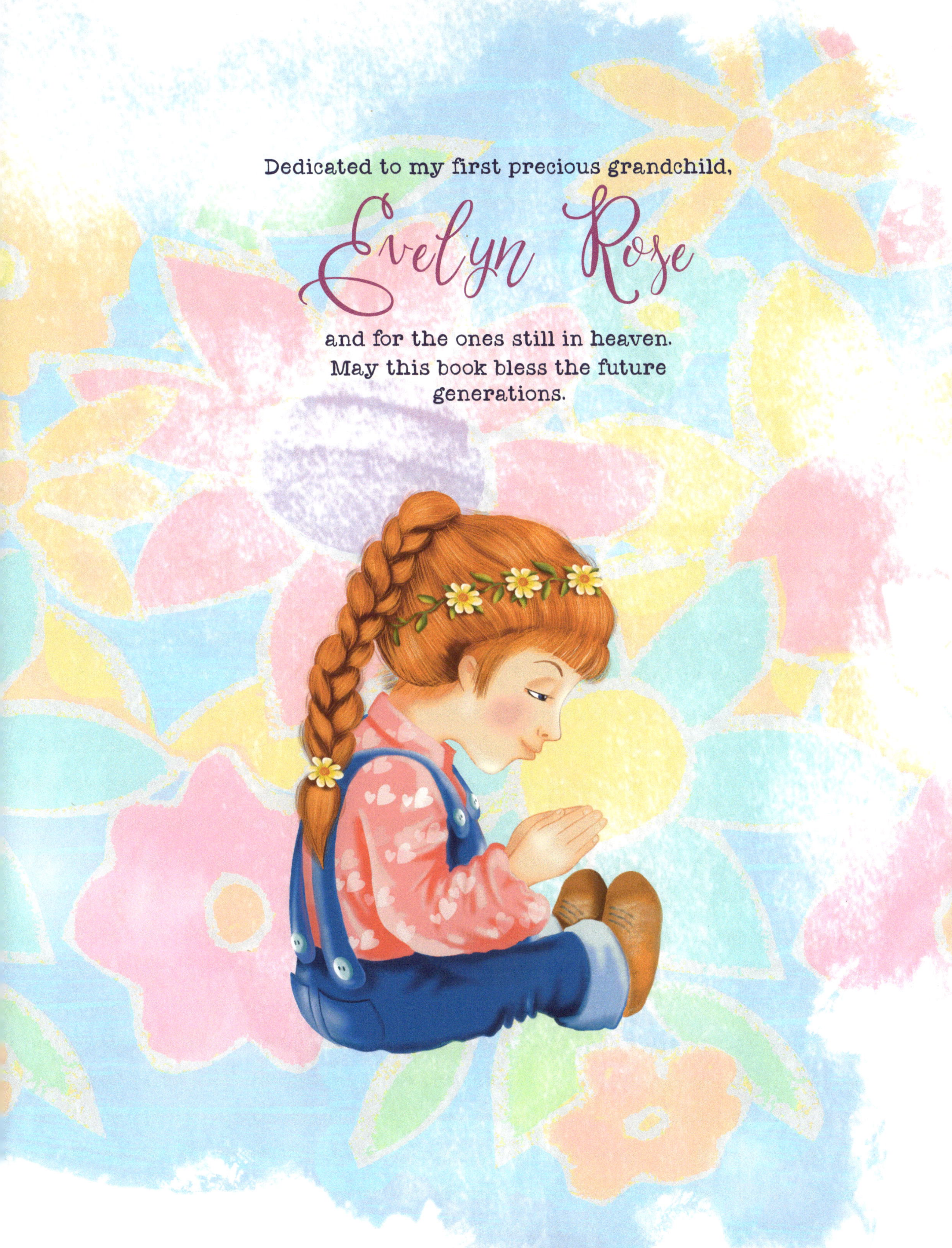
Dedicated to my first precious grandchild,
Evelyn Rose
and for the ones still in heaven.
May this book bless the future
generations.

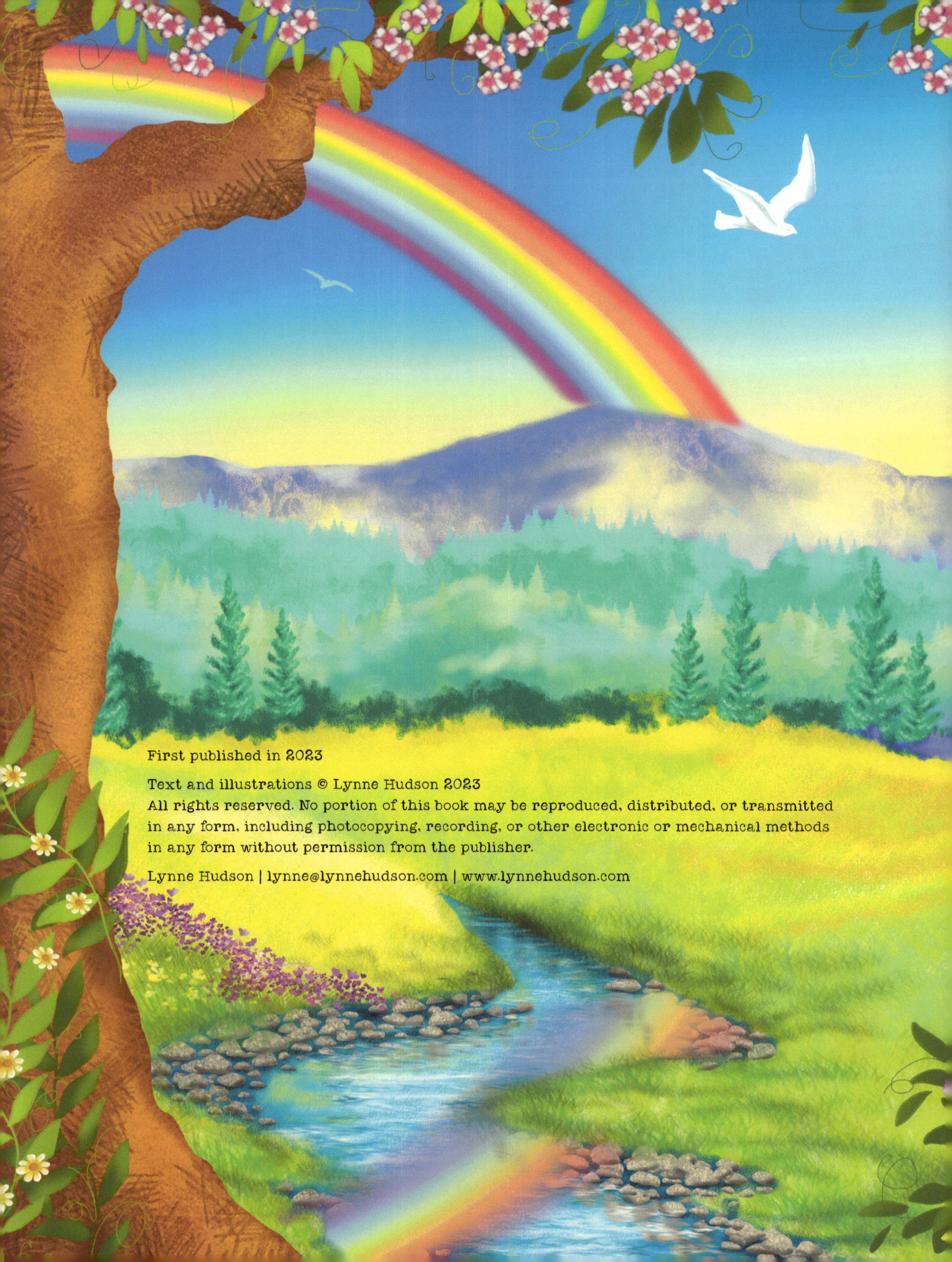

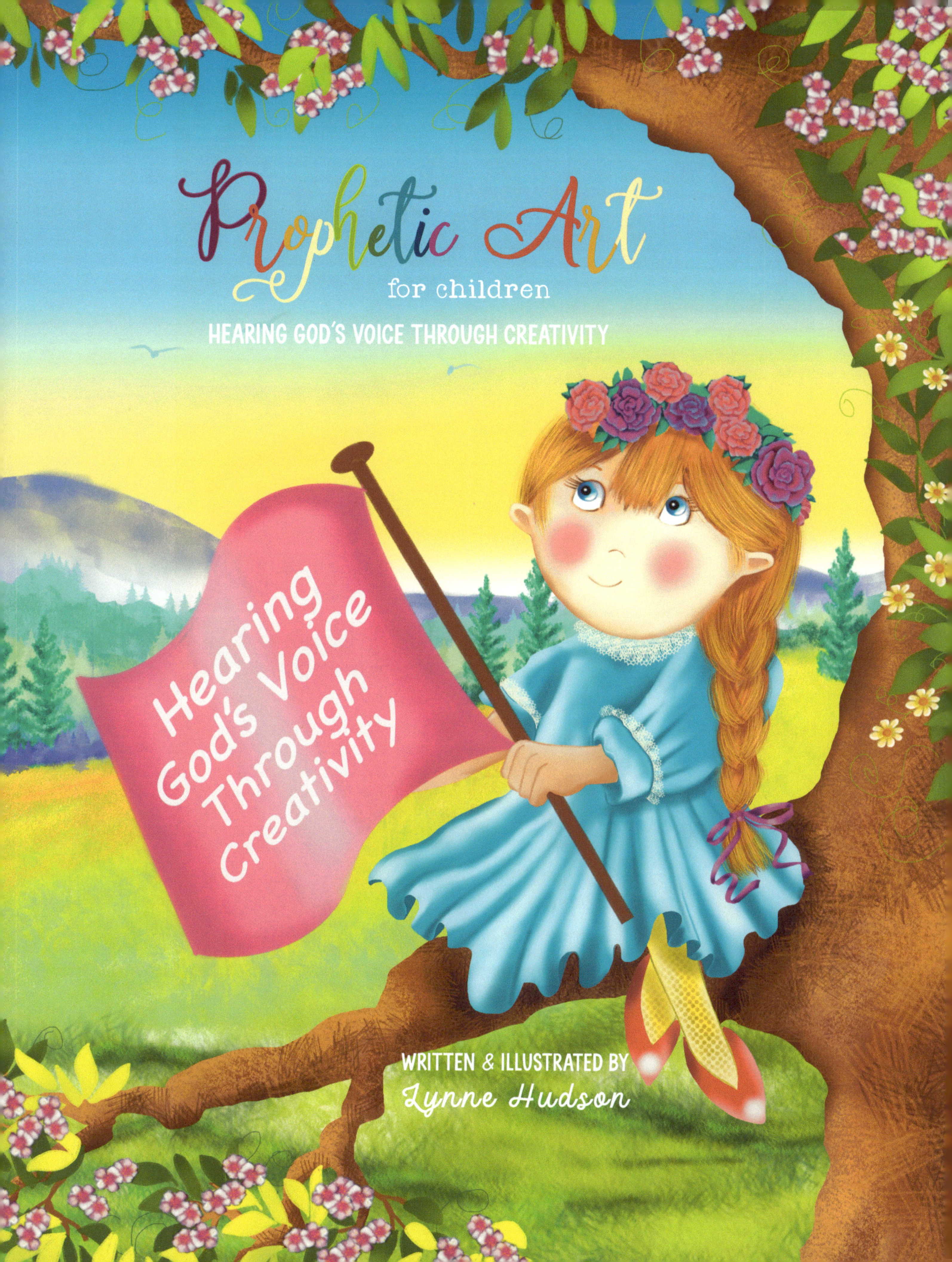

Prophetic Art
for children
HEARING GOD'S VOICE THROUGH CREATIVITY
Hearing God's Voice Through Creativity
WRITTEN & ILLUSTRATED BY
Lynne Hudson

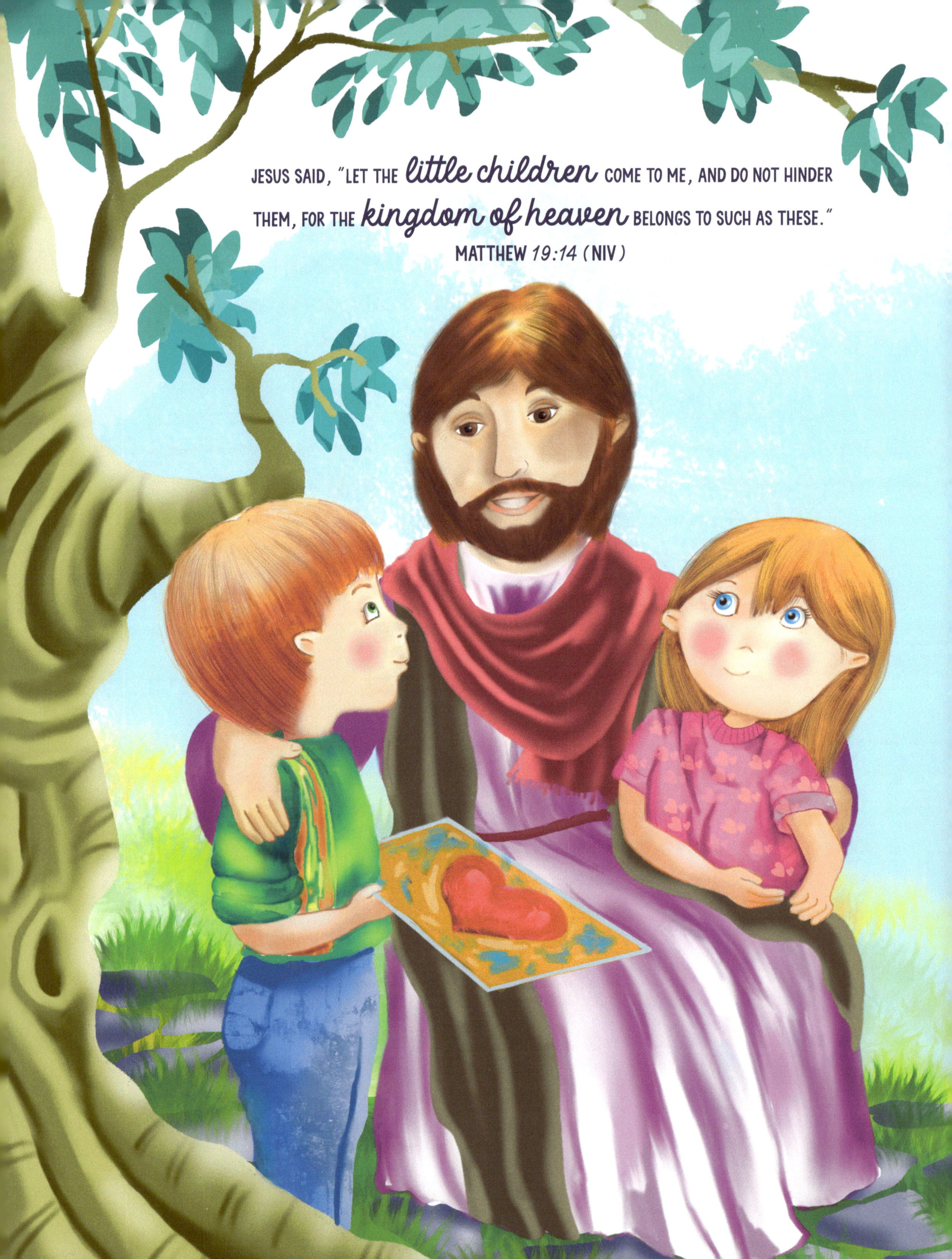

JESUS SAID, "LET THE *little children* COME TO ME, AND DO NOT HINDER THEM, FOR THE *kingdom of heaven* BELONGS TO SUCH AS THESE."
MATTHEW 19:14 (NIV)

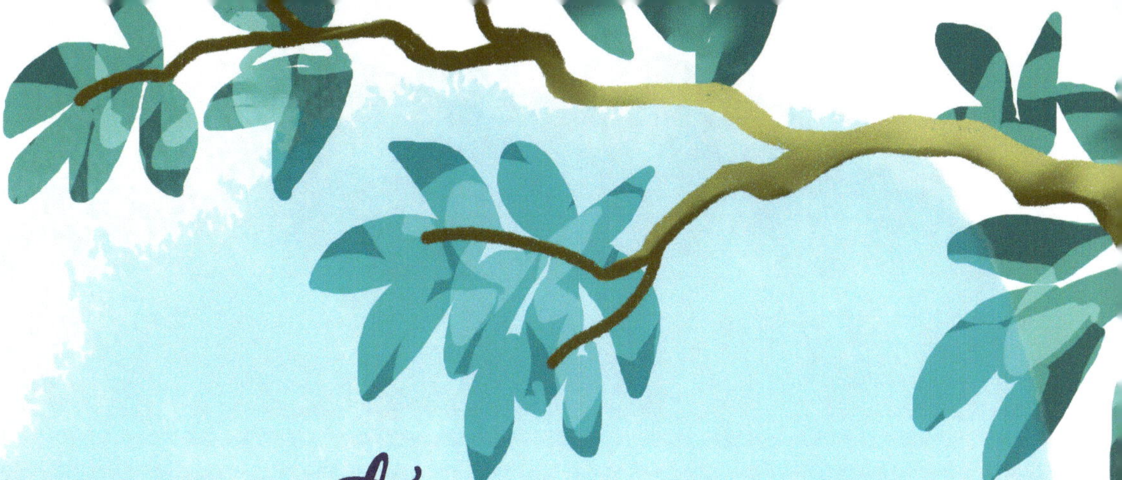

# Dear parents,

I pray that as you take your children through these pages that their hearts swell to hear from God in extraordinary ways. I have intended for this book to be an awakening of their minds and hearts to comprehend that God speaks to them in so many ways. Once they explore their creative side, this will open doors for them to see Jesus throughout their day. It sets them on a beautiful creative path to know that they have a friend in Jesus, whom they can rely on and ask questions to. They will feel the love of the Father and deepen their relationship with Him as they explore this creative medium.

Please read out the encounter to them or play my audio. After they have finished their paintings, discuss with them what Jesus is saying to them. Let them explore their paintings, looking at all the detail and colours to uncover even more of what Jesus was saying through their creations. What scriptures come to mind for them that relate to their creations? Ask them if the painting is for someone else. Join in if you can, so you can share your paintings with them as well.

May you be blessed as you work your way through this book.

Blessings and love,

Lynne

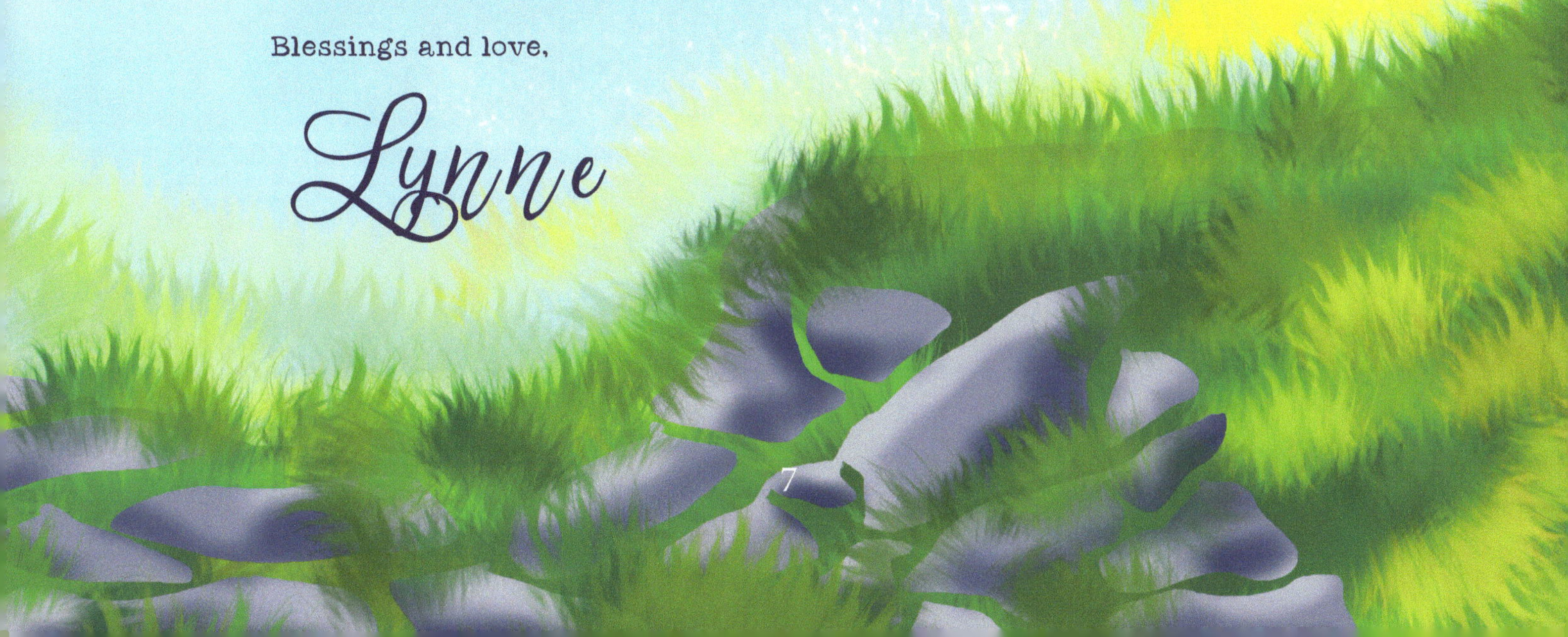

# What is prophetic art?

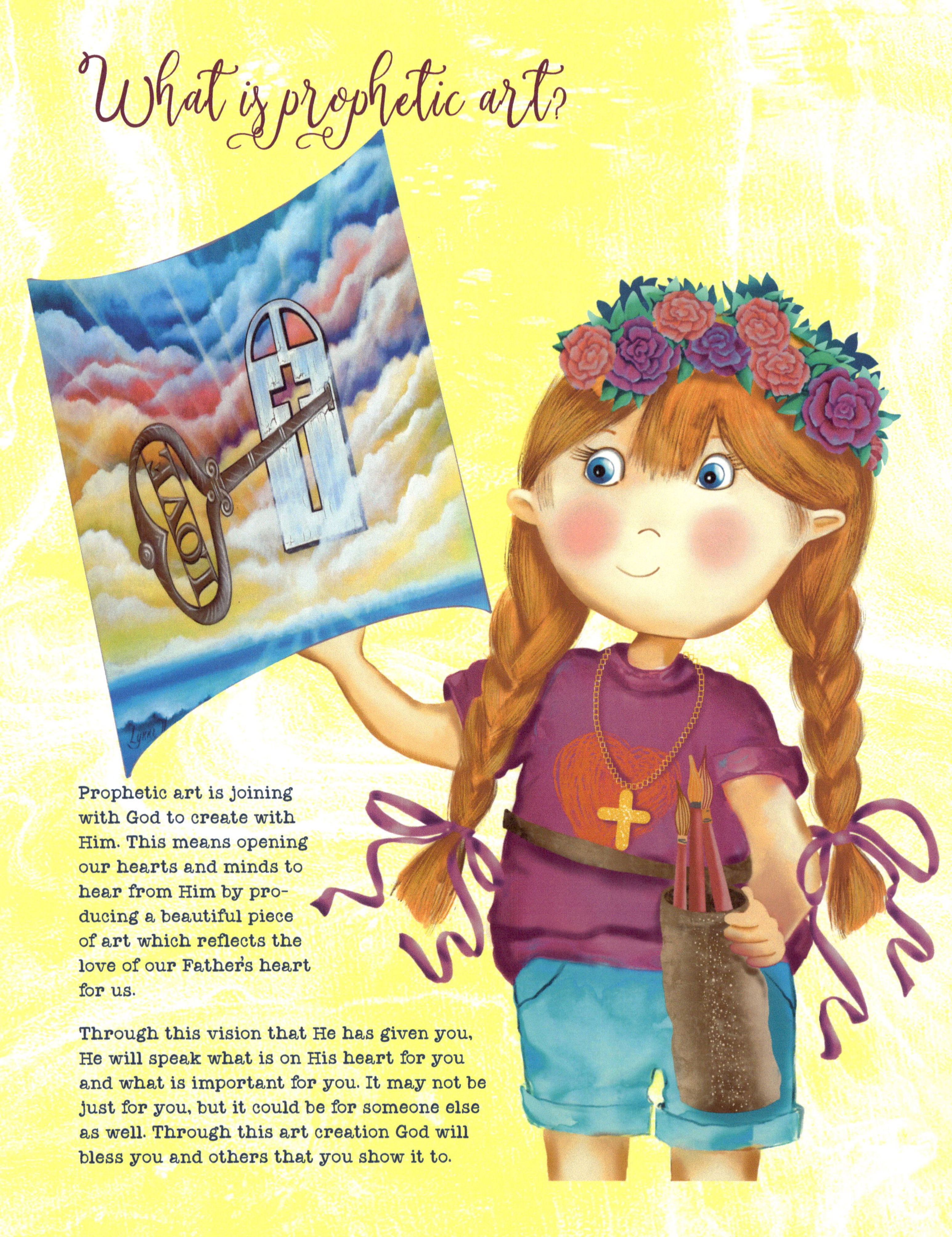

Prophetic art is joining with God to create with Him. This means opening our hearts and minds to hear from Him by producing a beautiful piece of art which reflects the love of our Father's heart for us.

Through this vision that He has given you, He will speak what is on His heart for you and what is important for you. It may not be just for you, but it could be for someone else as well. Through this art creation God will bless you and others that you show it to.

# I have always loved colour...

and to create by drawing and painting. From a very early age I discovered painting and would spend many hours creating whatever was on my heart—pages and pages of art. I loved to keep painting and not worry if I made a mistake but just to experiment with paint and brushes and water. To just have fun. That's what it's all about. Having fun. The more I painted the better I became as an artist.

If God has given you a gift, treasure it, develop it and work on your gift so that you can use this gift for how God intends to use it. He specifically chose you for this gift and you are perfectly made in His eyes.

So, what are your dreams? Are you creative? Do you love to draw and paint?

When we dream with God, He teaches us different ways to hear from Him and as you listen, you hear His heart. How wonderful that you can create with your heavenly Father.

God is the most amazing creator and artist. Look at the beautiful sunrises, and all the beauty around you, the flowers, the birds. There is so much richness in God's creation and we are created in God's image and we get to create with Him.

God loves all the arts, not just painting, but music, worship, books, dance, drama, writing, movies and cooking. He uses all of these mediums and more to talk to us. To reach out to us. God loves us so much.

I'm going to take you through encounters with Jesus in this book and we are going to practice creating with Him and hearing what is on His heart.

Creating with God is a beautiful way of knowing what He would like to tell you. You might have a question for Him and He will show you Himself through your painting and drawing.

Through our creations on paper, God will take us on a journey, a very intimate journey of what He would like us to see and feel from Him. You might need more joy in your life, so God might show you to paint a rainbow and this will represent all the promises He has for you. This brings you hope which brings joy. You may want to paint for someone to pray God brings healing into their body, so you might paint a picture of them fully healed. You can manifest your faith in God by making it a reality through your art.

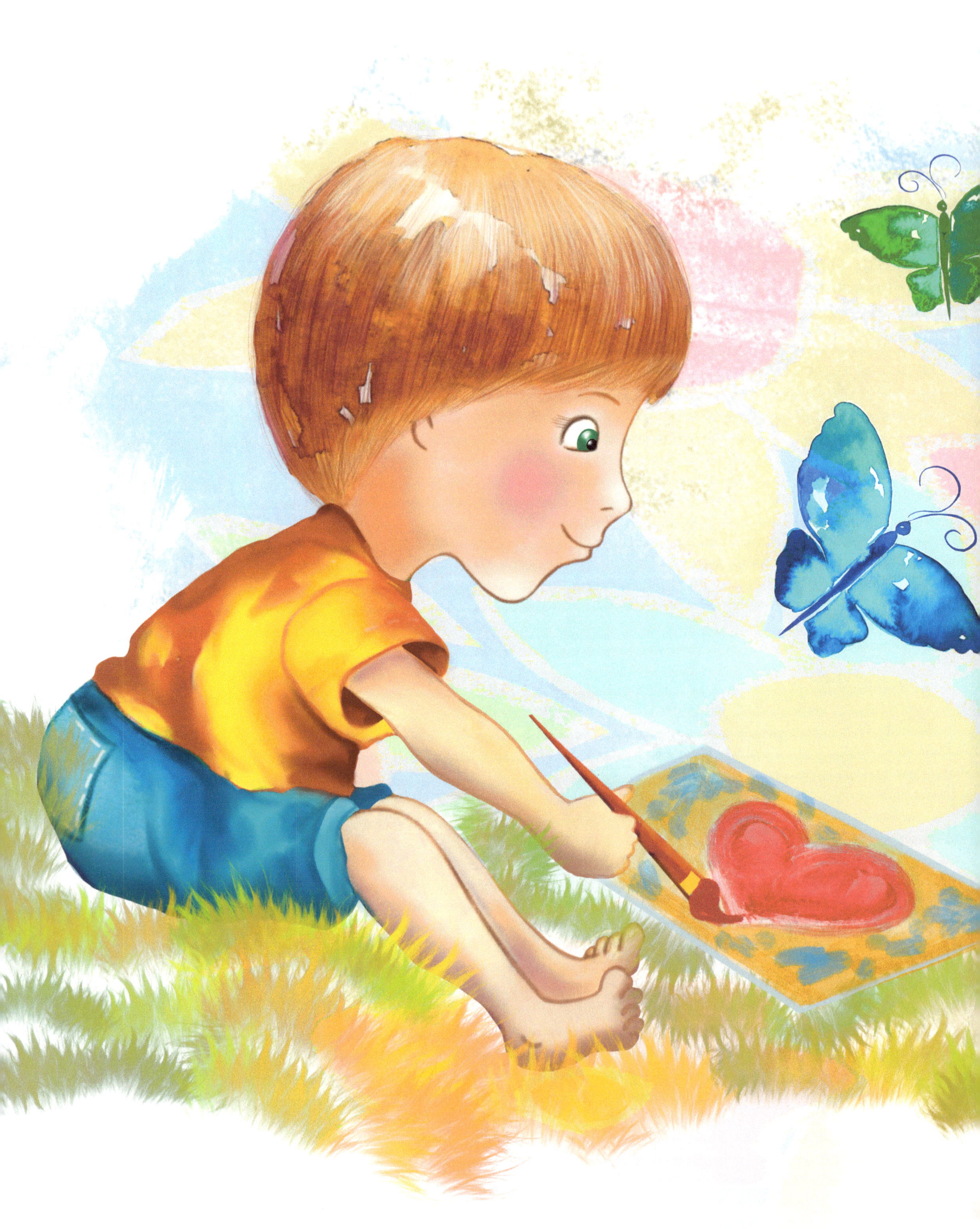

# It's always important...

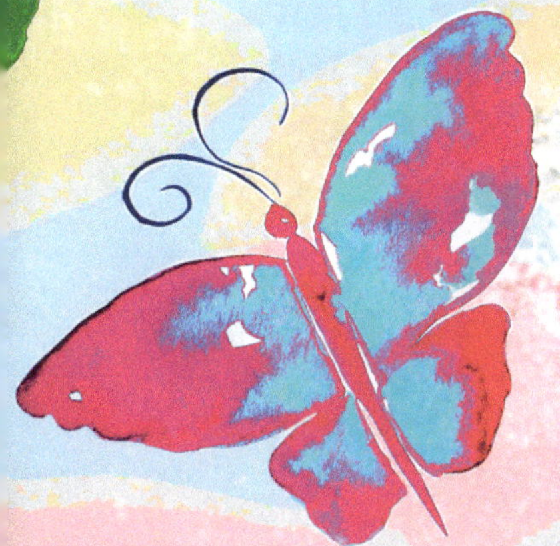

to just relax in God's presence, open your heart to receive from Him, and He will bless you. And it's also important to have a quiet space with no noise or interruptions. This allows us to settle ourselves before we begin our creative session with Jesus.

## Five Steps to Follow

1. **Quiet** yourself and find a stillness. Listening to instrumental worship music can help.

2. **focus** on an image of Jesus that He is with you.

3. **flow** with Jesus' thoughts.

4. **create** with Him.

5. **write** and journal what you feel was on Jesus' heart for you. Then ask the question—what is He saying through your painting?

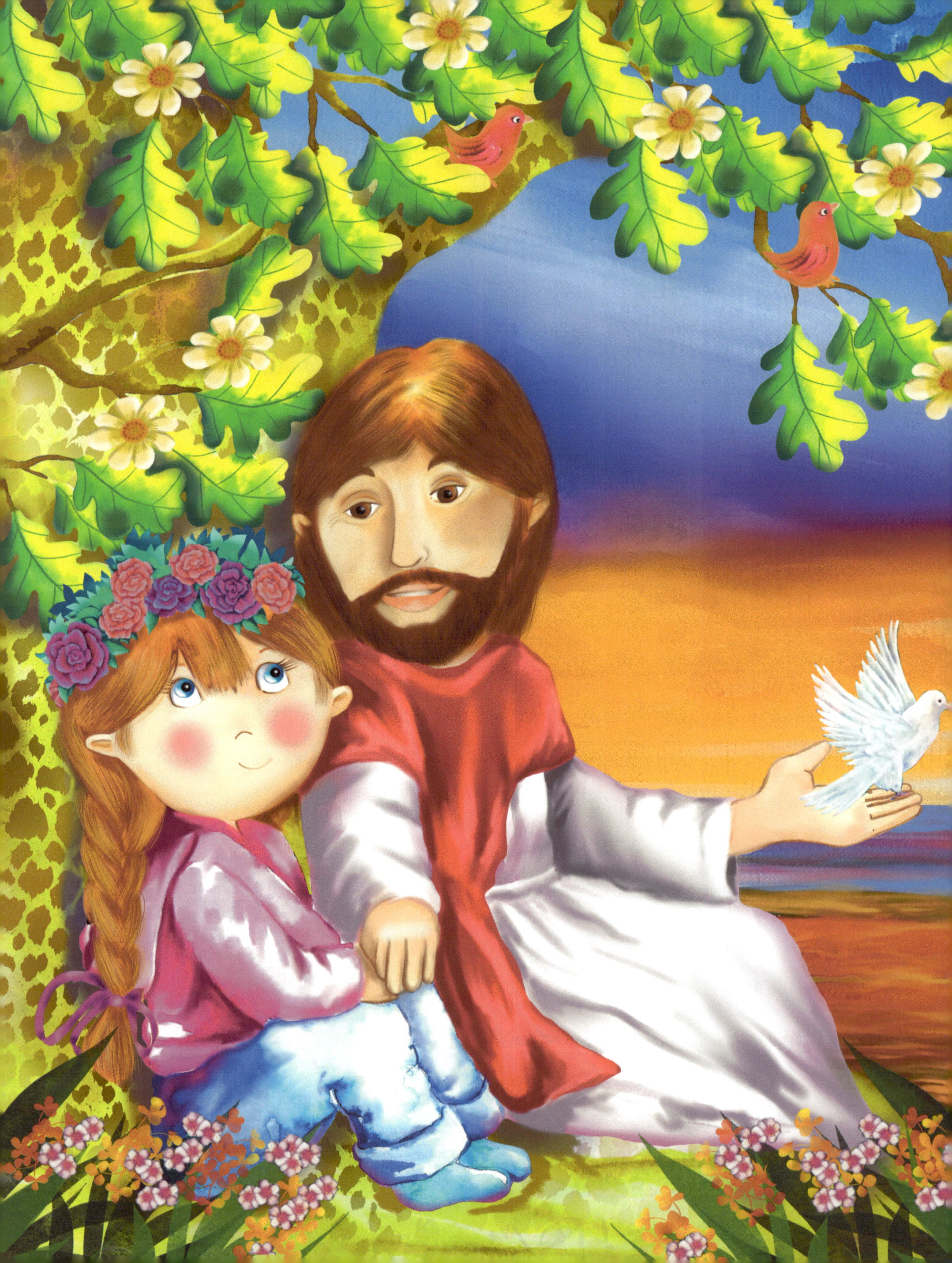

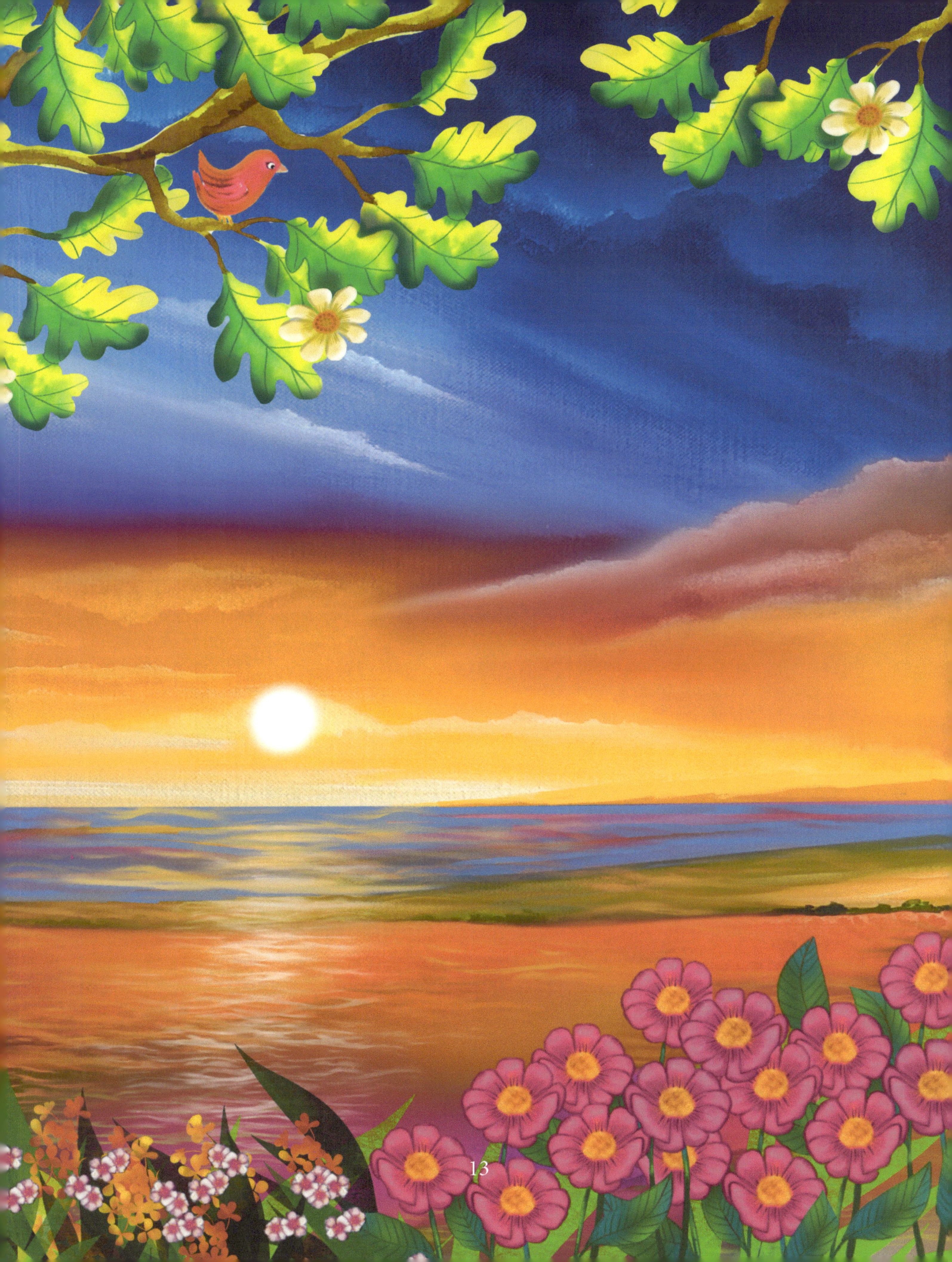

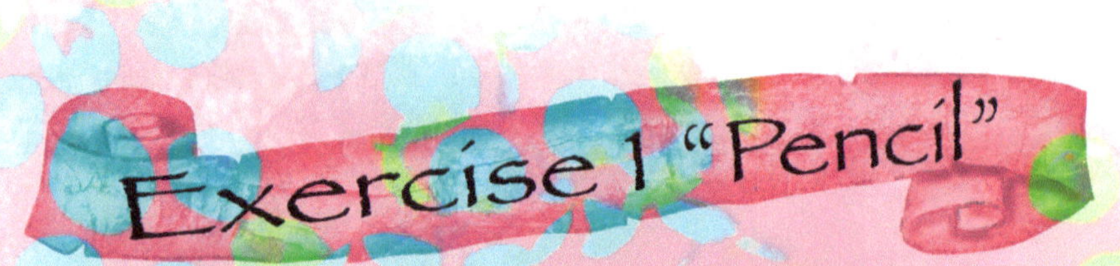


For this exercise we will be using a pencil only. We will be drawing with our eyes closed. Position your paper and hand with your pencil on the paper ready to draw when the encounter is finished. Ask Jesus about every part of your drawing. Look at the shapes, the lines, the scenes you draw, the people. What is Jesus saying to you through this drawing? Relax and don't worry about anything around you.

Pick up your pencil and place your hand in the middle of your paper. Close your eyes. Having your eyes closed while you draw means you aren't worrying about your drawing but imagining what God is showing you. You can make it a little bit more detailed later.

# Close your eyes and take a deep breath.

Relax and listen to the instrumental music that is playing. Take a deep breath and another deep breath. Now we will use our sanctified imagination and go on an encounter with Jesus. We are going to take a walk through the most beautiful garden. As we wander around this garden, I want you to look into your imagination and see what is all around you. Do you see beautiful flowers, an assortment of flowers? Do you see sunflowers reaching up to the sky? Do you see colourful perfumed roses? Can you smell the roses? Their perfume is from heaven. There are so many different flowers. Can you see them? Look around this garden. There is so much beauty because God made this beautiful garden. There is a huge oak tree. Can you see the beautiful bark on the tree? Look up into the tree and into the canopy of all the branches and leaves. See the patterns they are making against the sunlight as it streams down. Now you feel someone come alongside you. It's Jesus, and He is so excited to be with you. Wow, He's come to spend this time with you, just you, and no one else. He holds your hand and you go for a little walk around the garden path. It's a beautiful cobblestone path. Jesus is with you and you start to look at all the colourful flowers. It looks like a beautiful painting. "Come for a walk with me," Jesus says. So you begin to walk through soft, green, long grass, and climb to the top of a hill. There you see another huge old oak tree and Jesus says, "Let's go and sit down underneath this grand old tree."

You sit down and He's holding your hand. He says, "Look out to the horizon. What do you see?" The ocean is shimmering with the sun shining down and He says, "There is so much beauty in the world, my beautiful child, so much beauty." You feel comforted and loved by Jesus and know that You are loved by your Heavenly Father, who created all of this beauty for you.

"What would you like to ask me?" Think about what you would like to ask Jesus. Or you could just start by asking Jesus, "What is on your heart today? What would you like to tell me?" So relax and listen to the peace surrounding you. There might be chirping birds in the trees or a soft breeze on your face as you gaze out to the sea. Listen to what Jesus has to say to you. Ask Him your questions, listen for His reply, and look for visions in your imagination.

Let's create with Jesus. Now with your hand on the paper, and eyes closed, start drawing what you feel Jesus is showing you. He might tell you to draw a vision. Just go with the flow. He is showing you. It might just be a shape. Start drawing this and start moving your hand as you feel to draw. Even if you're not quite sure what you are doing, just keep drawing and then when you feel you are ready, open your eyes. Add details to the drawing if you desire. Look at what you have drawn and ask Jesus to explain this drawing to you. Ask your parents what they see. Journal what you feel Jesus is saying through your drawing.

## Materials needed:

### PAPER & LEAD PENCILS

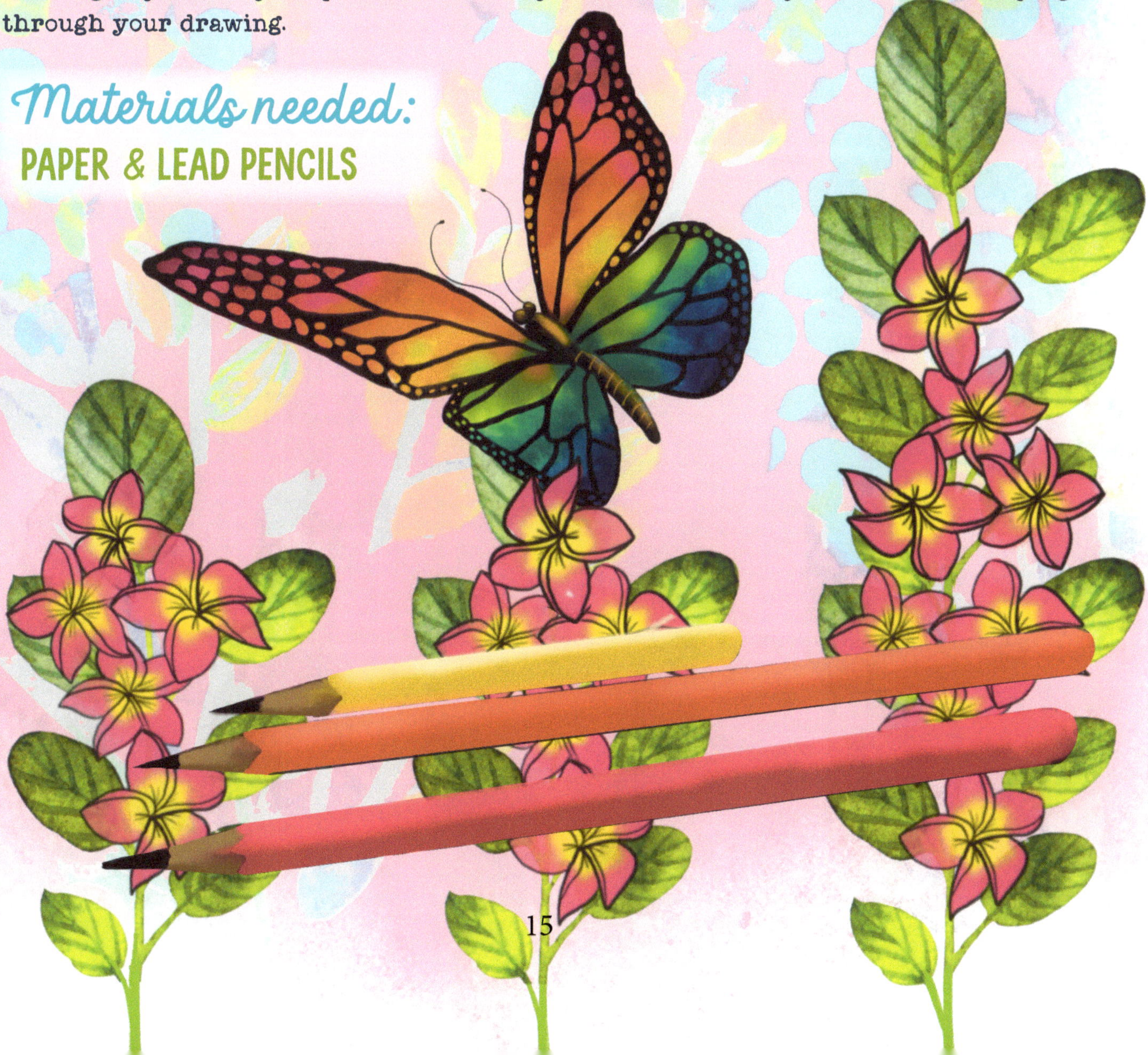

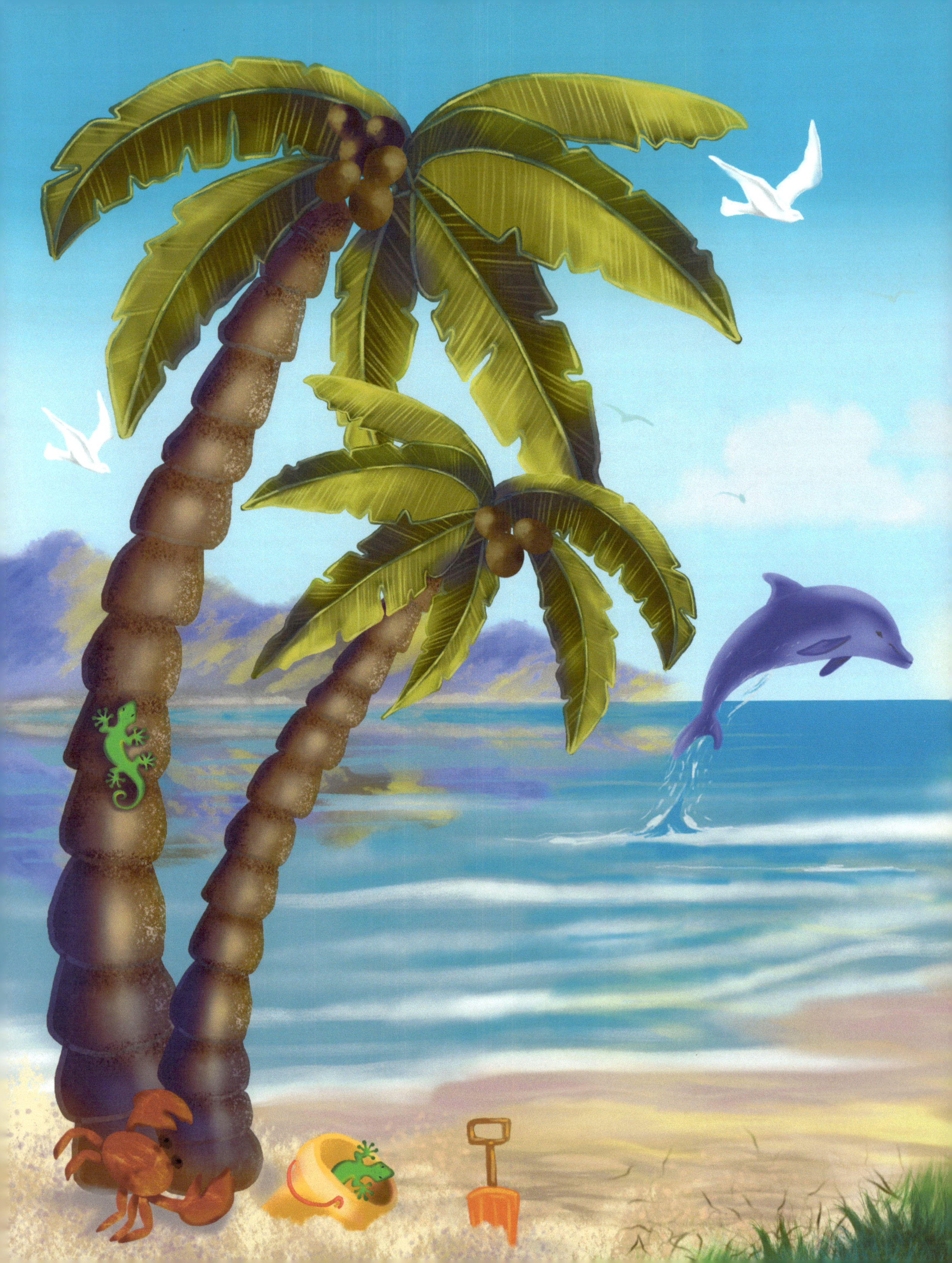

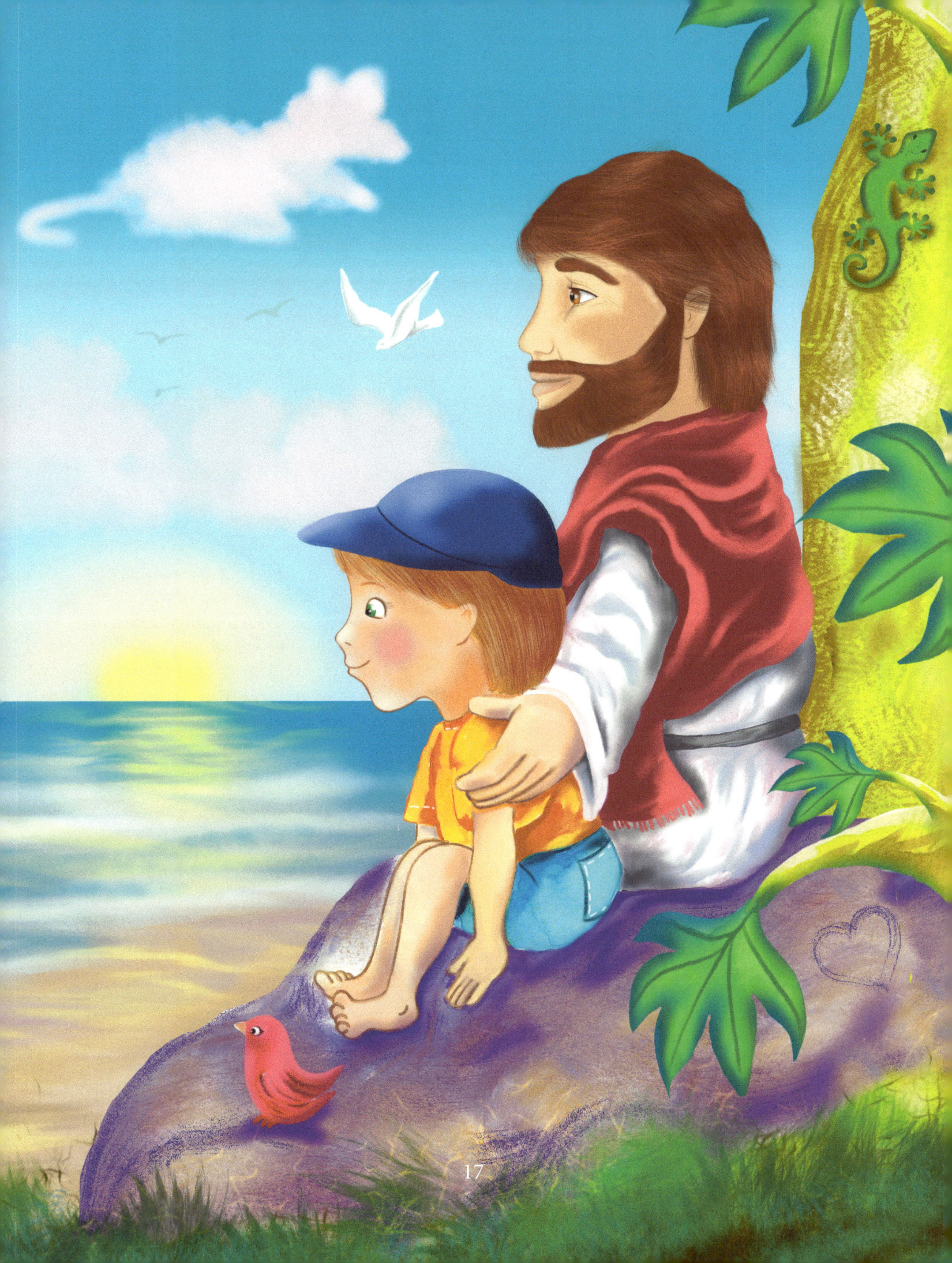

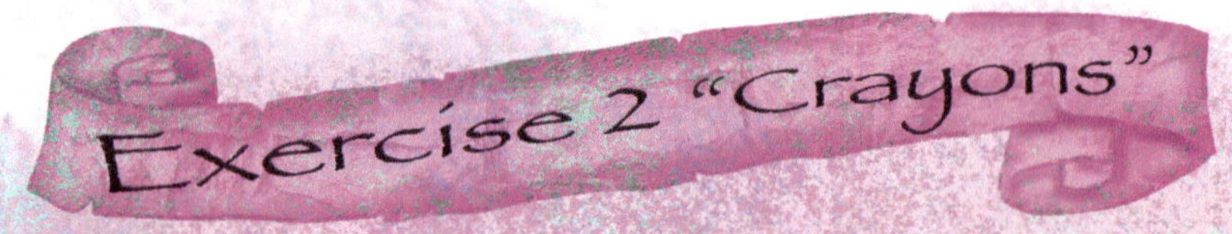


In this exercise we are going to explore with colour using crayons and coloured pencils. Every time you sit and spend time with Jesus, creating with Him, it will come more easily and you will feel His presence stronger each time. You have sacrificed this special time to be with Him and He will bless you through your art creations. We are using colour today.

## Ask Jesus,

"Why have I used this particular colour? You may have felt led to pick up a pink crayon. This represents joy and healing. Maybe Jesus is showing you that He is bringing joy into your life. Colour has so many meanings and we will explore this more in the next exercise when we use paints. I am going to take you through an encounter with Jesus and we are going to relax and let go of all of our worries, and not worry about what is going on around us. Get out your favourite crayons and coloured pencils or markers and some white paper. Ask mom to put on some instrumental worship music to softly play in the background. When we create today we will have our eyes opened.

Are we ready to encounter Jesus and listen to His heart so that we can create with Him? He wants to share something very special with you, something that is on His heart just for you. Listen to the music that is playing and take a deep breath. Relax your shoulders. Make sure you're comfortable. You may even want to put your head down in your arms on the table.

## Materials needed:
### CRAYONS & COLOURED PENCILS

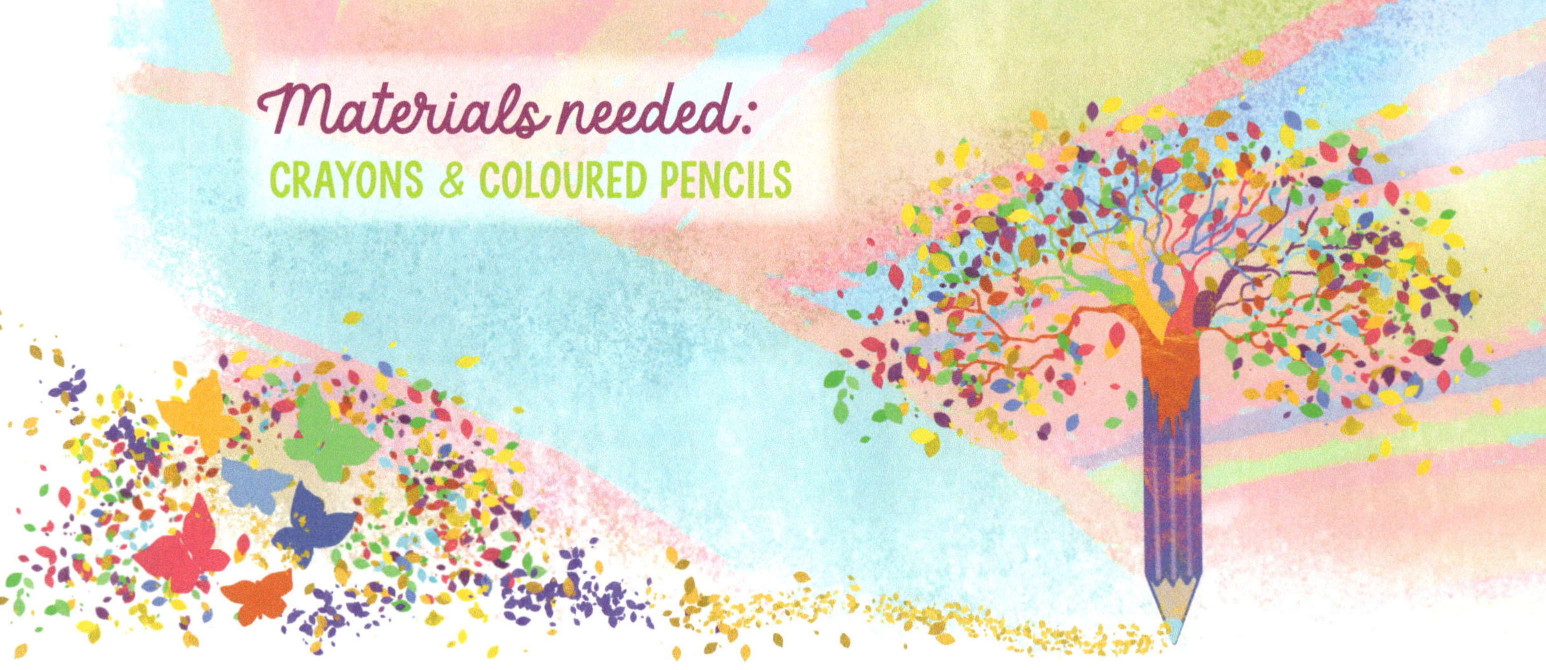

# AND WE KNOW THAT IN *all things* GOD WORKS *for the good* OF THOSE WHO *love him,* WHO HAVE BEEN CALLED ACCORDING TO *his purpose.*

Romans 8:28 (NIV)

Use your sanctified imagination and imagine. It's a beautiful sunny day. It's not too hot. There is a warm breeze on your face. There are palm trees blowing in the breeze and as you walk onto the sand and reach the water's edge you feel the soft lapping water on your toes. You look out to the horizon. Can you see it? Can you feel the warmth of the sun on your face? It's just a perfect day. You smile with happiness as you walk along. You are joyous, skipping along the water, making a splash, and then Jesus comes alongside you and He's so excited because He's with you. He holds your hand and He says, "Let's go for a walk." Walking along the beach, you feel the water splashing against your knees and you are jumping and dancing with joy with Jesus. You come to rock pools and you and Jesus explore the wonder of the small sea creatures that nestle in the water. What do you see? The colours and shapes are all unique. Do you see any crabs? Are there palm trees on the beach, swaying in the breeze? What else can you see? Are the clouds moving slowly in the sky? Is there a touch of pink? Can you make out any shapes in the clouds? Jesus and you have a game of guessing what you see in the shapes of the clouds. You are having a fun time. You're laughing and Jesus says, "Come with me, my precious child. Come and sit on the rock with me." You look out to the beautiful water and see the gentle waves just rolling in. There are seagulls flying through the air. Jesus says, "It is so special to be with you right now. I want to share my heart with you and tell you things. Do you have any questions for me?" Ask Jesus what you would like to ask Him or if you don't know what to ask you can ask Him, "What is on your heart for me, Jesus? Can you show me a vision for us to create today?

Listen to what Jesus says to you. Do you see a vision? Do you feel led to pick up coloured pencils and start drawing? Listen with your open heart and start to draw, making your picture as detailed as you like and even using all the colours if you wish. What do you feel is the message in your drawing? Journal the message. What do you see in your drawing? Did Jesus give you a vision to draw? Ask Jesus to tell you about what you have drawn. Let Him share with you the message in your drawing. What colours have you used? Are they bright and happy?

This is a beautiful, intimate, creative way to spend your prayer time. Date your work and keep them in a journal. You'll be surprised how God will speak to you through your creations, not just today but for weeks and years to come. Ask your parents for their interpretation of what they see. Is this drawing for someone else besides you? Do you feel led to give it to someone for them to be encouraged today?

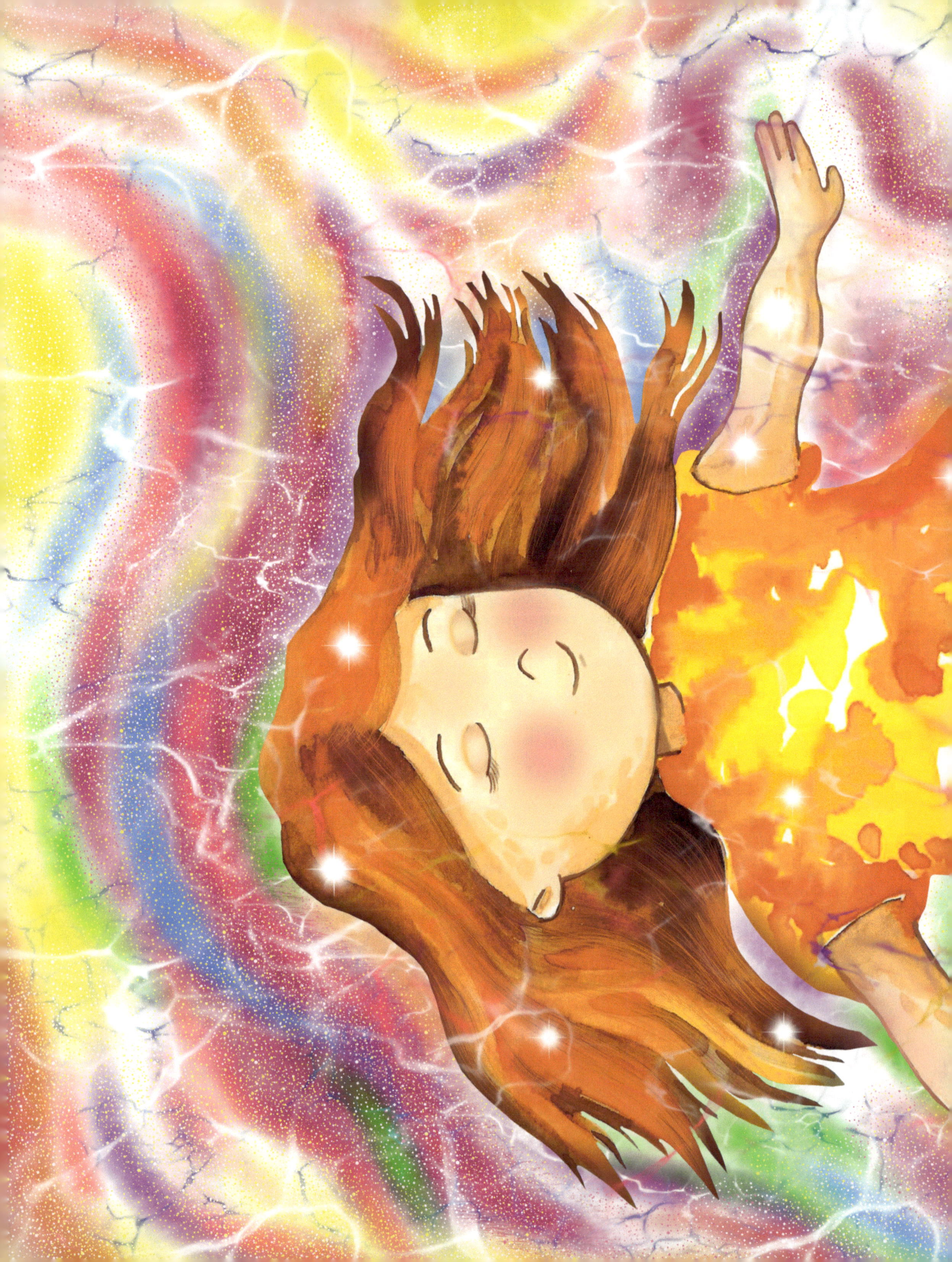

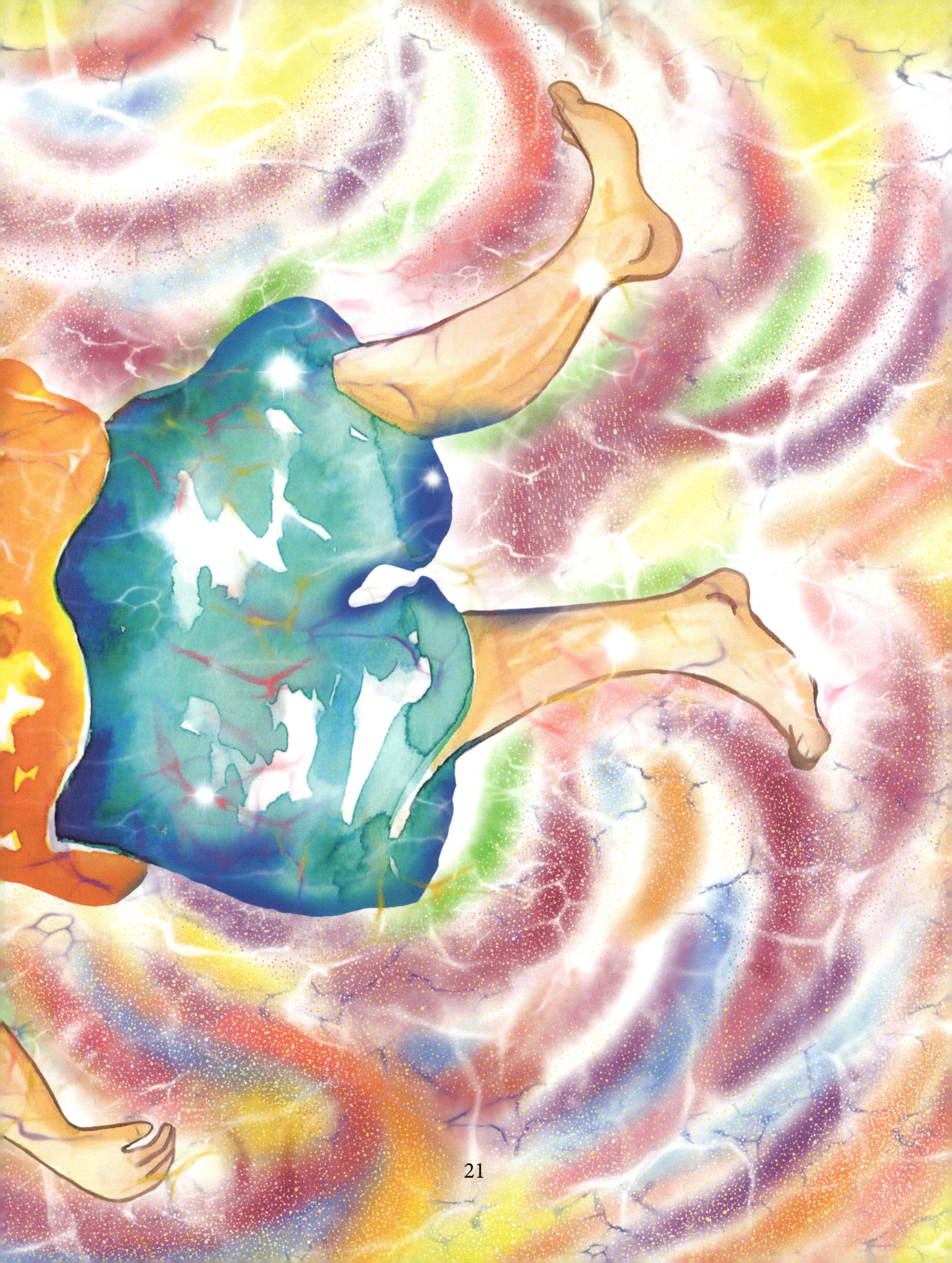

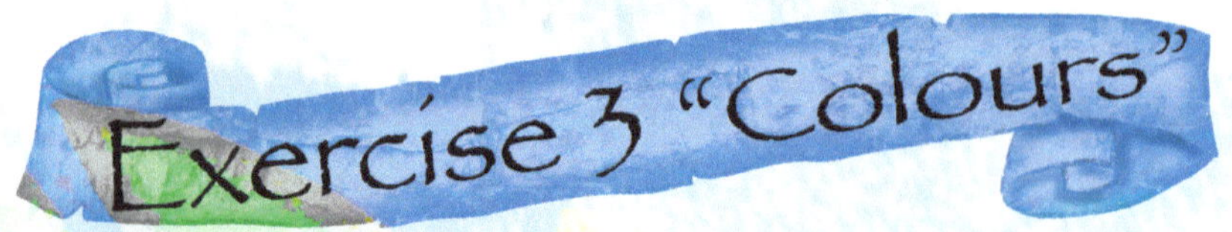


For this exercise we are going to paint with Jesus. Painting is so much fun. This will be different from using crayons and pencils. There will be more freedom of colour, more splashes of colour and not so much detail. We will flow with the liquid colour and see where our painting takes us with Jesus. When we paint, there is a freedom with the movement of our arms as we swish around the colours and blend the different tones using water to move the colour. There is a freedom to our creation more so than when we were using the pencils and crayons.

## Colour is everywhere.

I would like to explain to you about colour. Prophetic colour. Colours have so much meaning and because of this, God highlights your painting, your vision with Him, through the colours. Colour is so important to me. Doesn't it bring you joy? Our God is the most amazing artist of all time. He uses colour in everything that surrounds us. Just look at our sunsets and sunrises, tropical fish, tropical birds, flowers, rainforests, rainbows. Colour is everywhere. Every colour represents a meaning from God. This is why they are called prophetic colours—colours from God. When we look at a rainbow there are 7 colours. The rainbow represents God's promises. In the rainbow there are God's prophetic colours. Let me explain the meaning of prophetic colours to you.

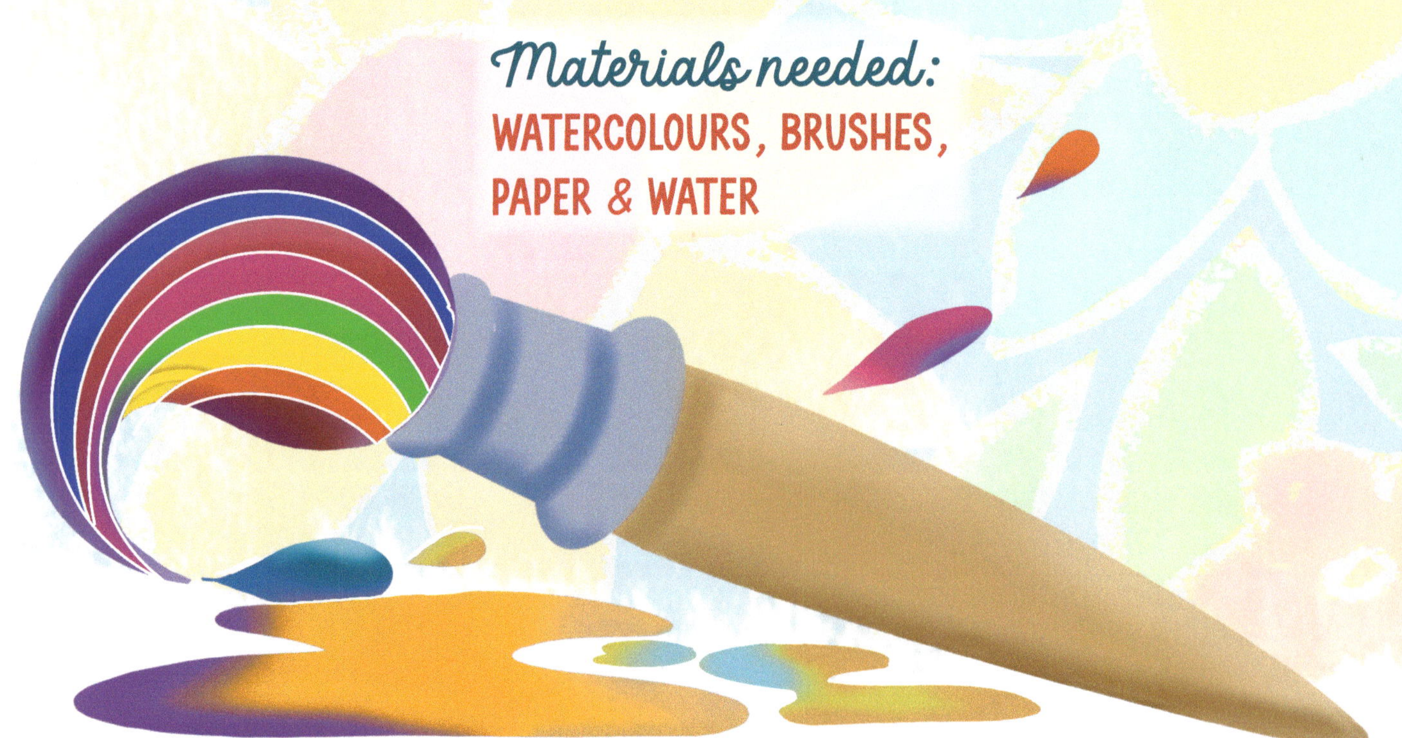

# Prophetic Colours

**Purple**: His royalty, our righteousness in God as we are part of His kingdom

**Blue**: The river of God, His refreshing living water, healing

**Red**: Love, The blood of Jesus, His sacrifice, redemption

**Pink**: Healing and joy, friendship with God

**Green**: New beginnings, growth, hope, happiness, birthing

**Yellow**: The glory of God

**Gold**: Fire of God, His glory and majesty

**Orange**: Courage, passion, fire and strength

**White**: Purity, holiness, peace

**Burgundy**: Blessings, rejoicing, the blood of Jesus

**Black**: Depths, mysteries of God, the secret place

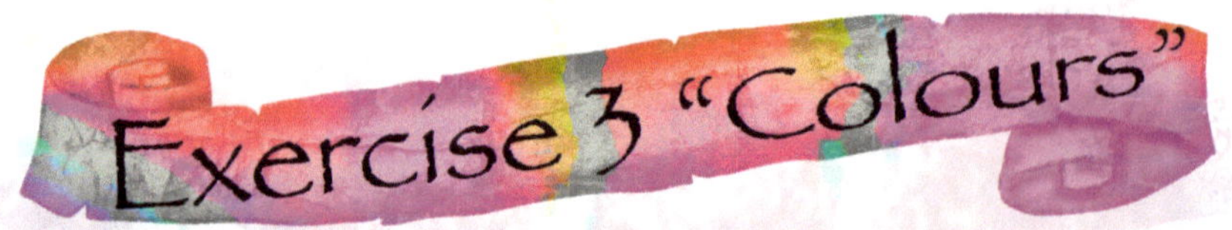


When I am painting with God, the Holy Spirit guides me to pick up a certain colour because not only is the vision of what I am painting very important, but so are the colours. Are you ready? Listen to His heart so you can create with Him. Close your eyes and take a deep breath. Relax and listen to the music that is playing. You are walking up a big hill and there are long, soft green strands of grass all around you. At the top of the hill there is the most beautiful big oak tree, an incredible big oak tree that is enormous. You sit under the tree. Jesus comes along and sits down next to you and you are so happy and so excited that He's come to sit with you. He is spending this time with just you. Jesus holds your hand, and He says, "My beautiful child, look around you. Look at the glory I have created for us." Look at this oak tree. Look up into the branches. Do you see the beautiful green leaves, the birds sitting in the branches? Listen to their beautiful songs. Do you see butterflies flying in and out of the branches? Jesus says, "Look out to the mountains that are down by the river. Look at this river. It is crystal clear. Let's go down to the river's edge. You walk down while Jesus is holding your hand and as you walk down you are skipping and are so very happy. Gaze into the river. It's flowing. It's crystal clear and you can actually see right to the bottom. It's not very deep and Jesus says, "Let's jump into the river. One, two, three, jump!" You jump in and splash and it's so cool and refreshing and you're laughing and Jesus says, "I have a surprise for you," and you are so excited. You slide down and float in this beautiful river. You are feeling weightless and the temperature of the water is just glorious and Jesus says, "I want you to use your imagination and I want to show you the beautiful colours." He says, "Look at the colours, the rainbow colours."

# Colours start to flow into the river.

First comes a rich purple, which is the righteousness of God. God is cloaking you in a satin robe of purple and you're feeling like His beloved child. You feel so loved. Next comes the sapphire blue and the blue is so refreshing, it's Living Water. It's filling you up and it's healing you. Are there any parts in your body that need healing? In your heart or in your mind? Is there any sickness in your body? Receive that beautiful blue that's pouring into your body right now. Believe for healing. Next is red. Red is love, the blood of Jesus. He sacrificed His life for us. The red love is surrounding you and going into your heart. Next comes the pink. Oh, the happy pink, which is healing and joy. Can you feel the joy invade into your body? Can you see that beautiful, bright pink? Is there any more healing that you need? Receive that pink healing. Next comes the green. Vibrant bright green, which is the new beginnings and growth of hope and happiness. There's a new birthing, a new growth, which means you're getting rid of the old and you're receiving the new. You are receiving healing thoughts from Jesus in your mind and in your heart. Next is yellow, which is the glory of God. He is filling you up with His glory. It is pouring out and shining. Now the orange comes. This is the courage God gives you to step into the plans He has for you. Receive it. Now white, which is the purity and the holiness, peace and blessings. Imagine every single colour right now and the particular colour that you need. Imagine it is filling up your whole body, your whole mind, your whole heart. Jesus says,

## Relax in the anointing of my colours from heaven.

And as you float in His goodness, you are feeling incredibly loved, nurtured, refreshed, healed and protected in your heart. Now ask Jesus a question. Ask Him, "What is the message for me today?" He might remind you of what happened in the river and He might give you a vision of what was happening when you were floating in the comfort of His care. Ask Him, "What would you like to show me, Jesus?" Paint that vision and when you have finished, look at your painting and ask Jesus to explain even more about this creation. Listen to what He has to say. What colours have you used? Are there bright and happy colours, colours you saw in the river? Is there any dominant colour? What is the painting about? Ask Jesus. Ask your parents what they see. Journal your thoughts.

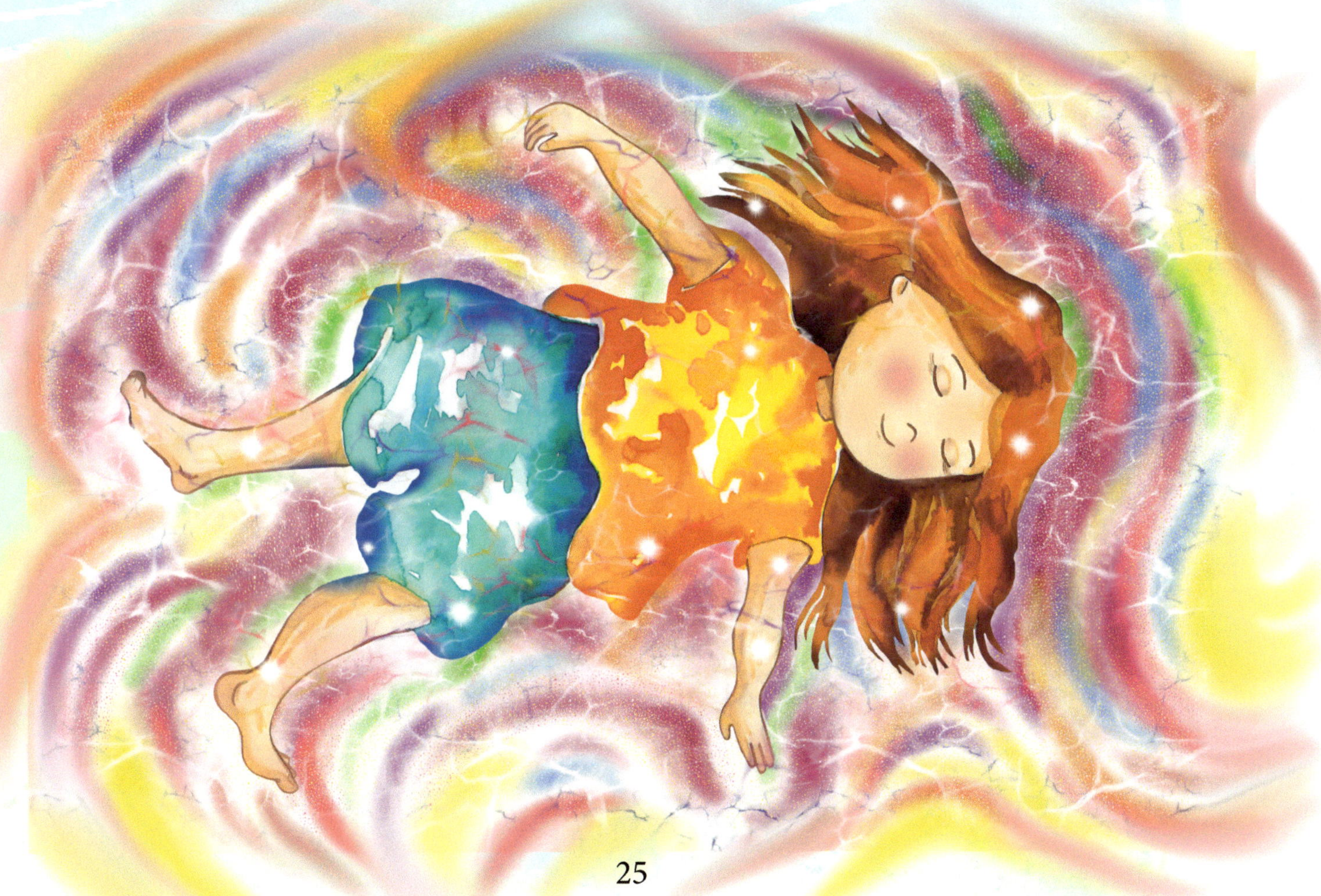

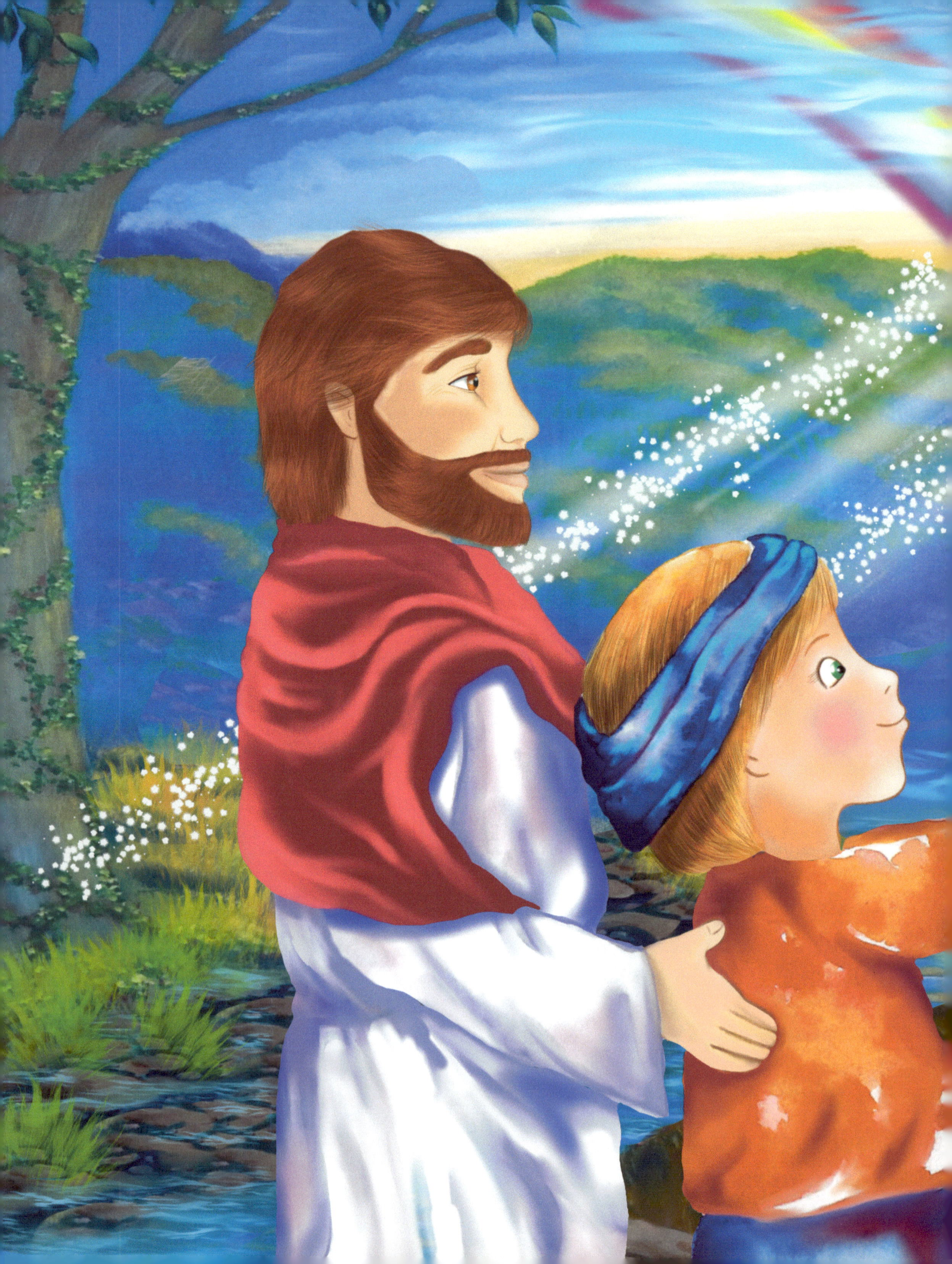

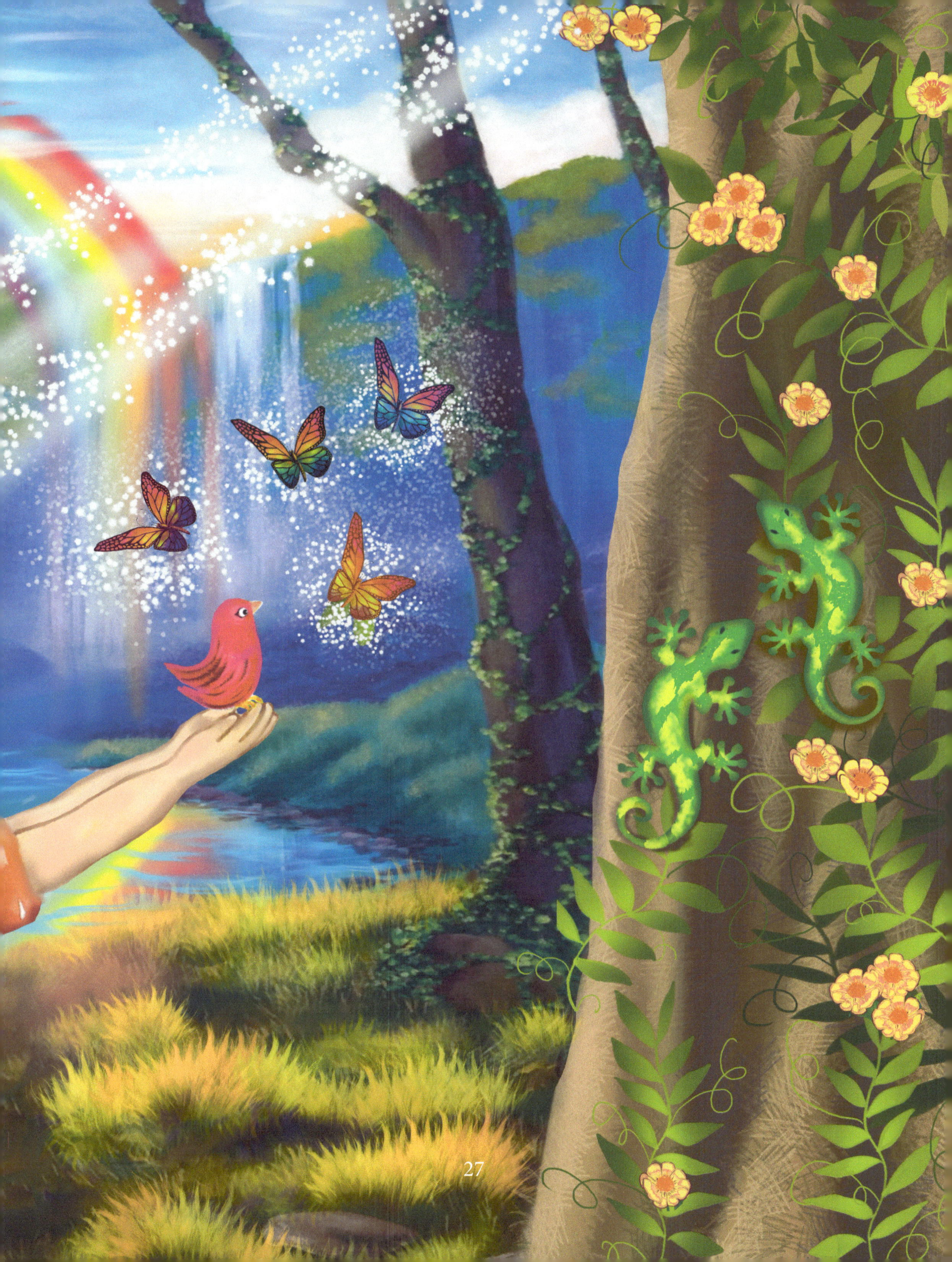

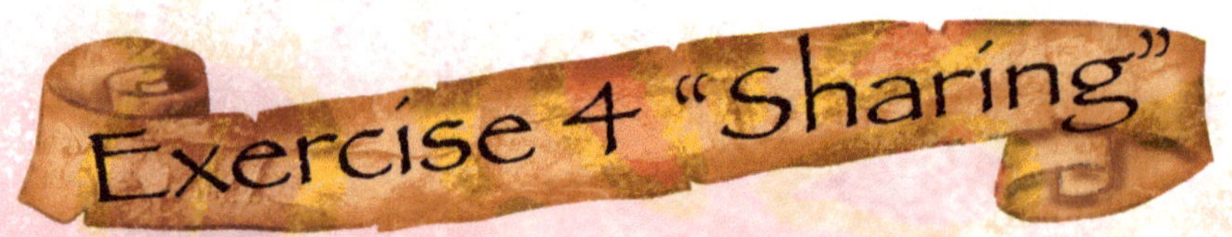


For this exercise you are going to paint a picture for someone that is special to you. It might be your mom or dad, someone in your family or a friend. It is always important that when you create a picture for someone it brings them joy and hope. You have already learnt from the encounters I have taken you through that it is important to still ourselves, settle down and be quiet. We imagine Jesus is with us and use our imagination to be with Him and ask Him questions. Through this we hear from Him and create what He has put on our hearts to paint. When we create a picture for someone and we have a message for that person from Jesus it blesses them. It gives them joy and happiness. Because you have taken the time to listen to Jesus and create a story just for them. It makes them feel so special. I am going to take you through an encounter with Jesus and we are going to relax and let go of all of our worries, and not worry about what is going on around us. Get out your coloured pencils, crayons, watercolours, brushes, water and some white paper. Use whatever medium you feel led to use. You might just feel like using the pencils, or all of your art materials. Ask your parents to put on some instrumental worship music to softly play in the background. When we create today we will have our eyes opened. Are we ready to encounter Jesus and listen to His heart so we can create with Him? Take a deep breath, relax and listen to the worship music playing. You are in an enchanting rainforest. Do you hear how still it is? There is the melodious singing of rainforest birds. They sing a heavenly tune, a melody from God. Look around you. What do you see? There is a gentle babbling brook that is meandering next to the path you are on. Look into the crystal clear water. Do you see the waterfall that is in the distance? There is a refreshing coolness upon your skin. Look up into the trees. Do you see the gorgeous colourful birds perched on the branches? The butterflies swirling around you? Do you see the sunlight pouring down through the criss-crossing of branches? This is God's glory shining down on you.

## Jesus is right next to you.

You are so excited that He is with you. He says, "Let's walk along the path next to the brook." Look around you. Do you see the beauty that I have created for you to enjoy?" You are so happy to be spending this time with Jesus. You go on a journey with Jesus and you both walk deeper into the rainforest. There are exotic colourful flowers all around you. Jesus says, "What would you like to ask me?" Ask Jesus, "Is there someone you would like to give a message to? Can you show me that person and can you show me the creation to make for them?" Ask Jesus these questions and listen to His heart. When you have someone on your mind and the vision that Jesus has given you, start painting.

# What do you see in your painting?

Did Jesus give you a vision to paint? Ask Jesus to tell you about what you have created. Let Him share with you the message in your painting. What colours have you used? Are they bright and happy? Is there any dominant colour? Look at the list of colours. Is there a stronger message in your colours from Jesus? You may get a fuller understanding of your painting from God by looking at the colours you have chosen. Write down what Jesus has said about your painting. What do you feel is the message in your painting? Ask your parents for their interpretation of what they see. Who is this painting for? Remember the painting should be uplifting and bring joy. Make sure a parent is with you when you give this creation to someone.

## Materials needed:
**WATERCOLOURS, BRUSHES, PAPER, WATER & COLOURED PENCILS**

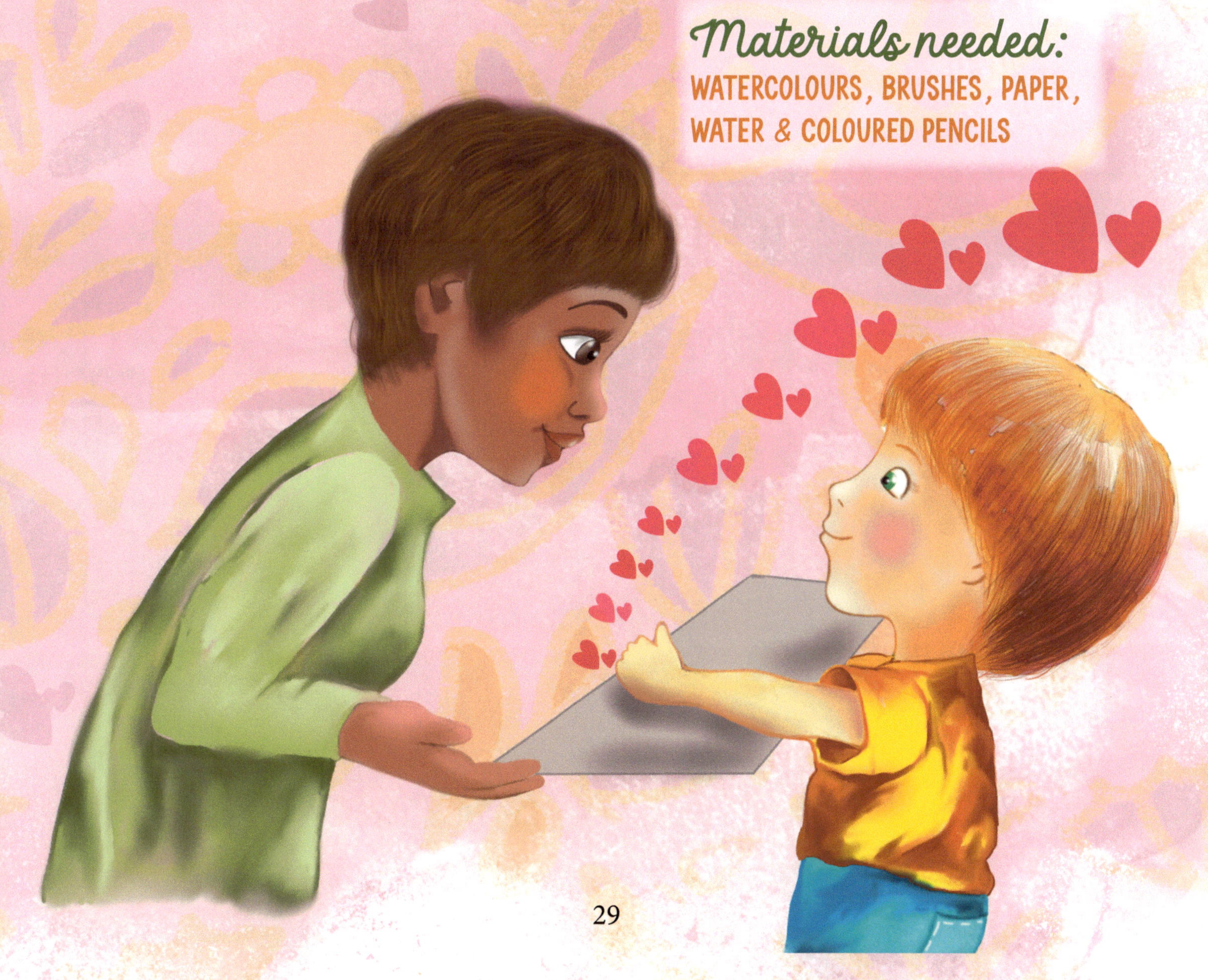

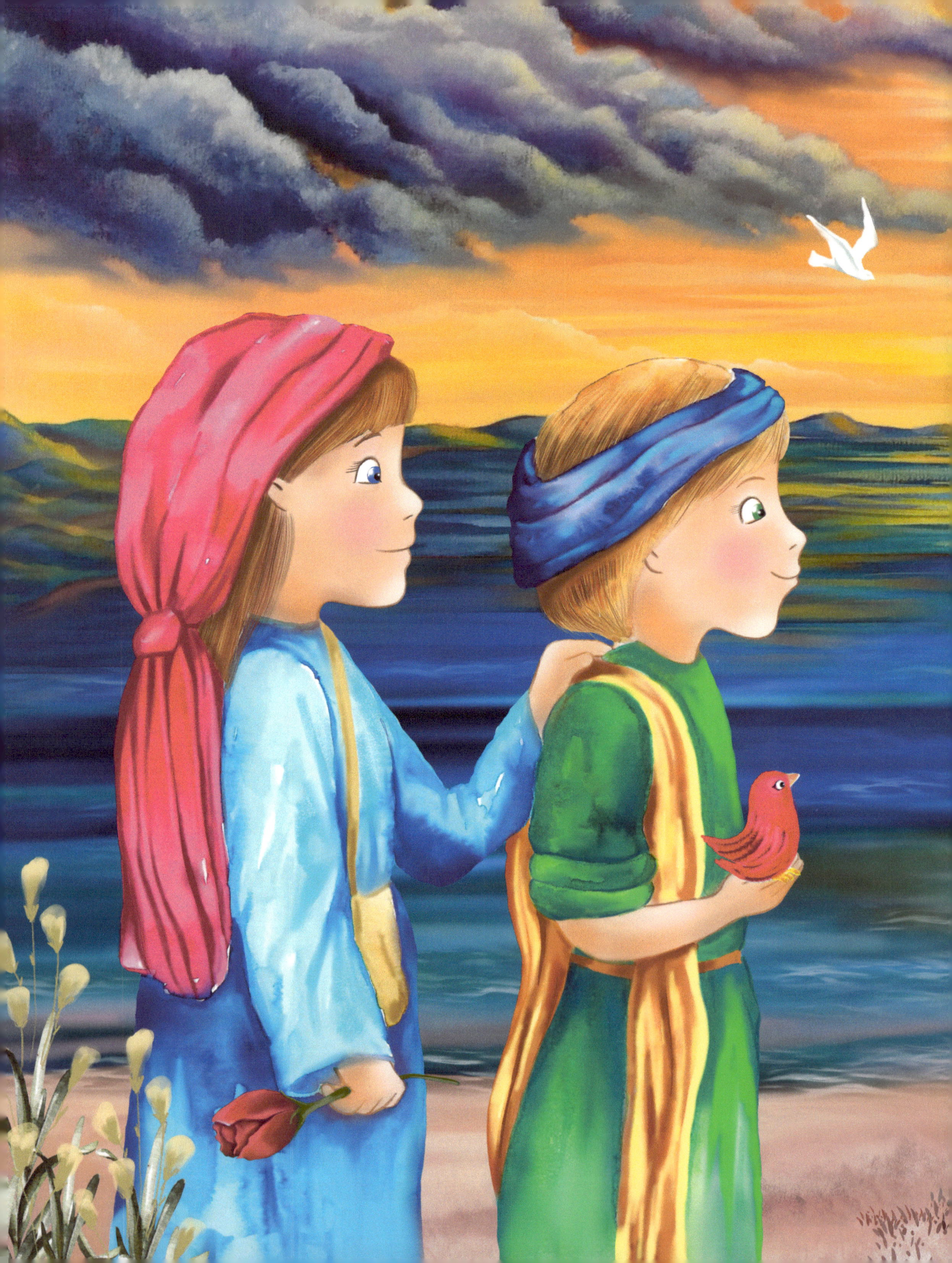

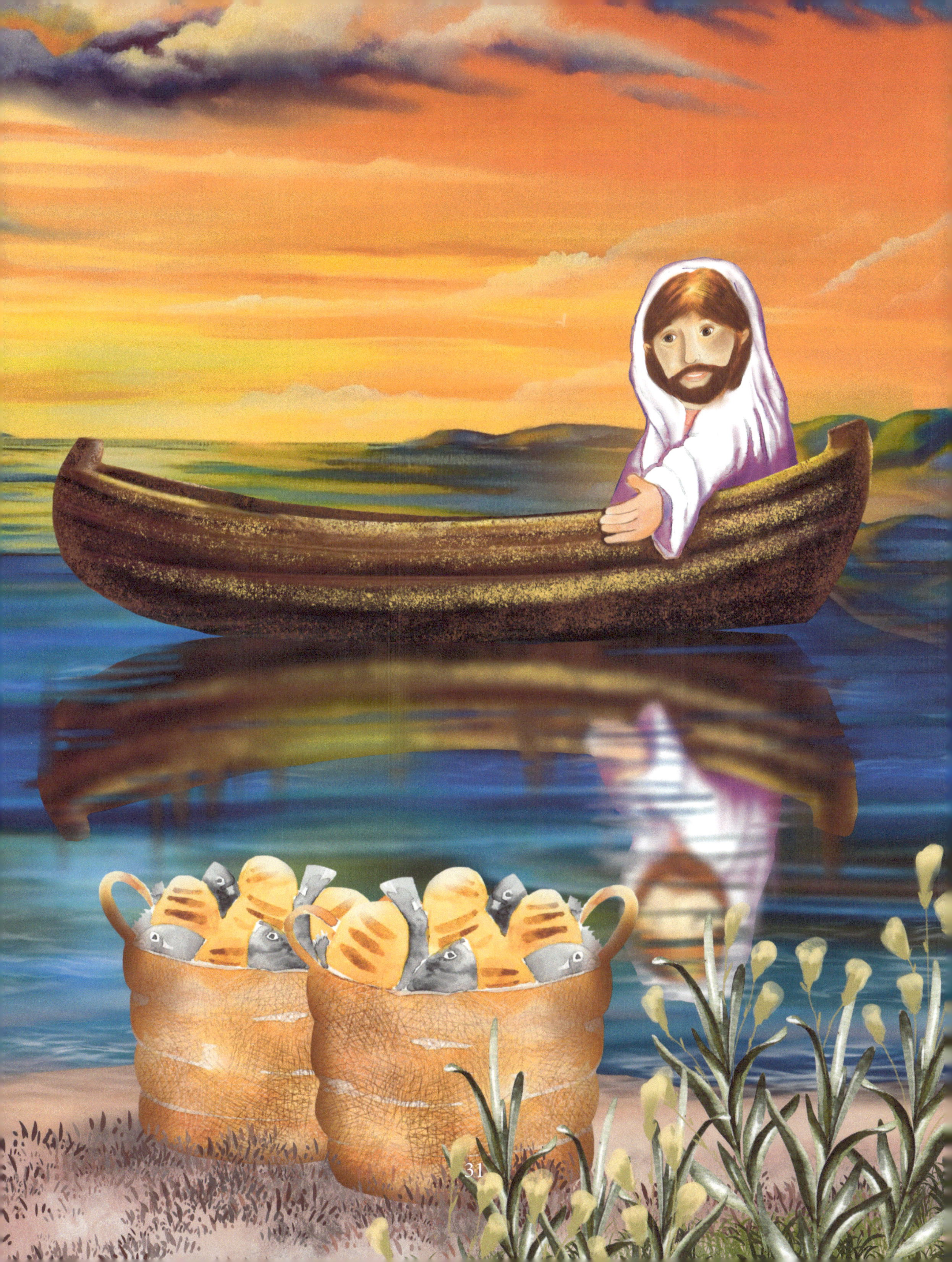

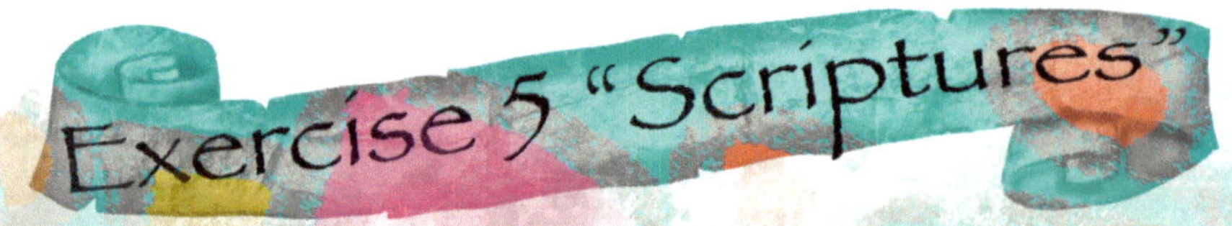


During this exercise I want you to use your sanctified imagination and take yourself into this scripture. With your paints ready, we are going to explore our surroundings in this encounter and feel the love of Jesus as we walk in biblical times with our Lord. Relax and take a deep breath, quiet yourself, close your eyes, listen to the music and step into this scene with Jesus. Imagine the clothes you are wearing are basic sackcloth, simple sandals and a headscarf. Sit down by the side of the lake and listen to this scripture.

*After this,*

Jesus crossed over to the far side of the Sea of Galilee, also known as the Sea of Tiberias. A huge crowd kept following him wherever he went, because they saw his miraculous signs as he healed the sick. Then Jesus climbed a hill and sat down with his disciples around him. (It was nearly time for the Jewish Passover celebration.) Jesus soon saw a huge crowd of people coming to look for him. Turning to Philip, he asked, "Where can we buy bread to feed all these people?" He was testing Philip, for he already knew what he was going to do. Philip replied, "Even if we worked for months, we wouldn't have enough money to feed them!" Then Andrew, Simon Peter's brother, spoke up. "There's a young boy here with five barley loaves and two fish. But what good is that with this huge crowd?" "Tell everyone to sit down," Jesus said. So they all sat down on the grassy slopes. (The men alone numbered about 5,000.) Then Jesus took the loaves, gave thanks to God, and distributed them to the people. Afterward he did the same with the fish. And they all ate as much as they wanted. After everyone was full, Jesus told his disciples, "Now gather the leftovers, so that nothing is wasted." So they picked up the pieces and filled twelve baskets with scraps left by the people who had eaten from the five barley loaves.

John 6:1-13 (NLT)

Jesus showed so much compassion for the people in this scripture. Do you show love and kindness to those around you? How can you help others? This young boy only had a meagre meal to share but he sacrificed his own comfort to help others. Jesus saw the love and generosity of this small boy's offer and multiplied it to help others. God uses sacrifice to shape the giver's heart and advance His kingdom.

Jesus uses the small amount we have to offer and multiplies it. Through your offering to help others by using your gifts, Jesus will go beyond what we feel we can do and use our simple offerings greatly. Listen to Jesus. Now ask Him what you can offer to others. How can He use what you have and multiply it to help others? Is it your gift? What miracles has Jesus performed in your life? It could be something very small and simple or something life changing. Think about all of this. Sit and listen. Then start to paint the visions He has for you. Feel His heart and create. Then journal His words. Discuss your painting with your parents.

## Materials needed:
**WATERCOLOURS, BRUSHES, PAPER, WATER & COLOURED PENCILS**

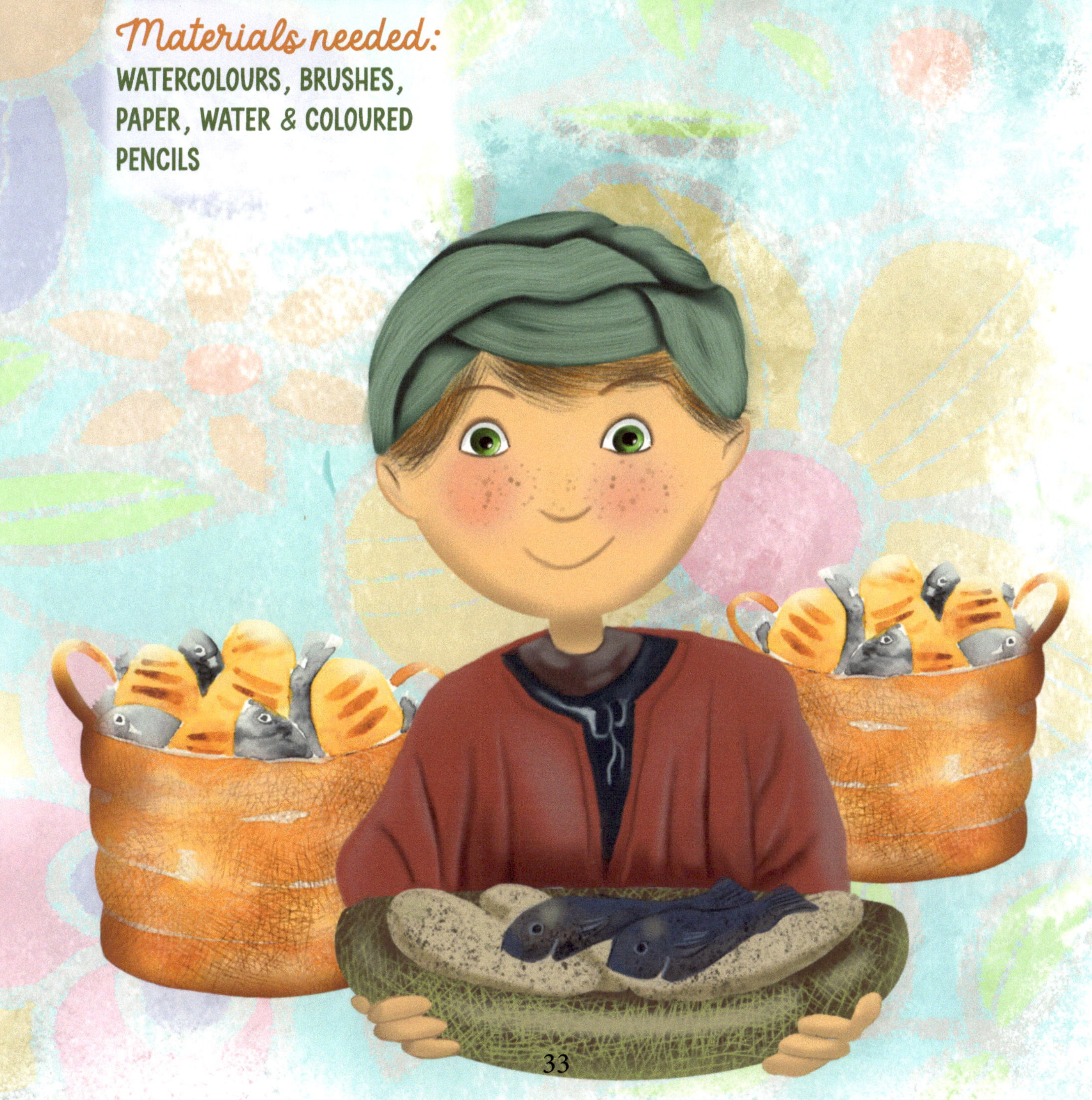

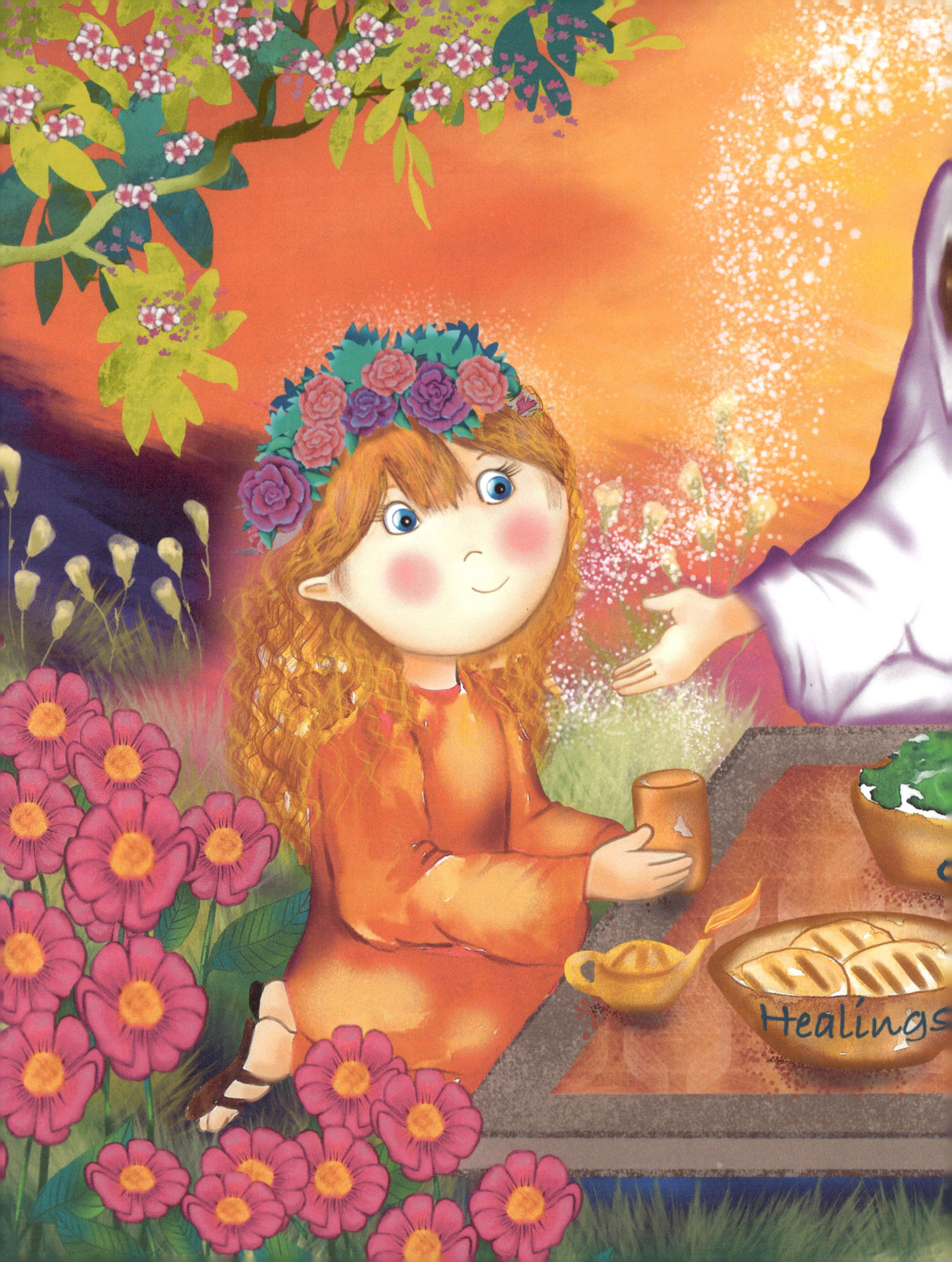
Healings

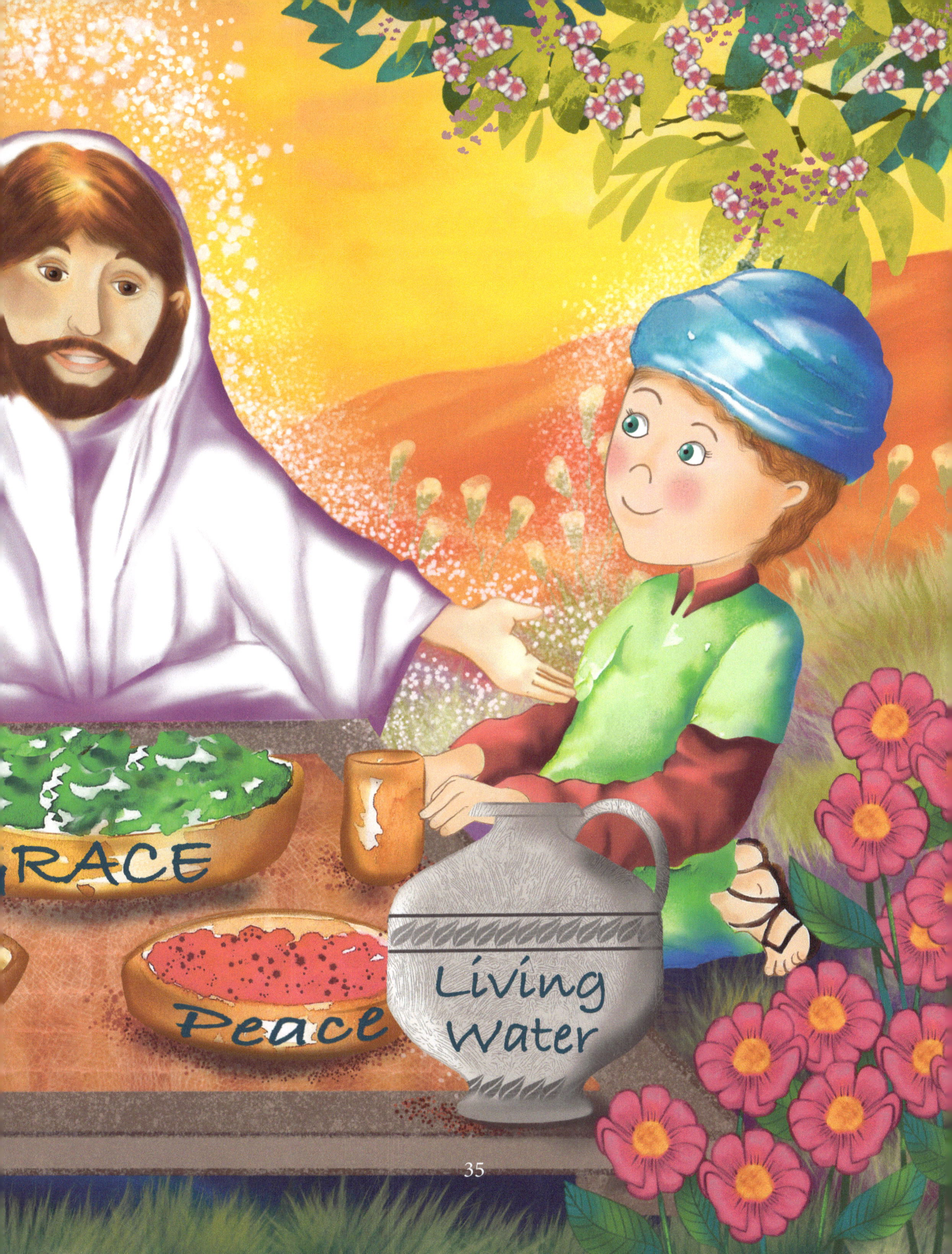
RACE
Peace
Living
Water
35

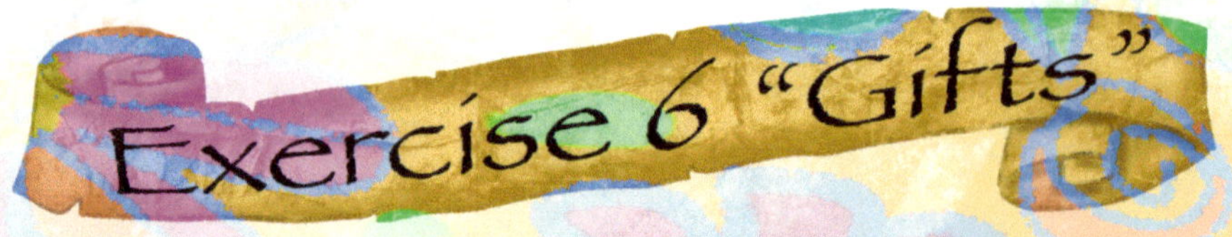


In this exercise we will listen to Jesus' heart on what our gifts and callings are. God has given you a beautiful gift, a purpose for your life. This purpose was written in His book long before you were born. Sometimes our gifts are obvious. I always loved art and this has been my gift from God to help people to know Jesus through my art. This gift could be called a talent as well. But I have used this talent for the purposes of God's kingdom. What are your talents and giftings? Do you feel called to do God's work?

## Let's ask Jesus about this.

When God gives you a gift, it is so important to honour this gift, respect it, and enhance this gift. This might mean taking lessons or studying to be better at your gift. I spent many years working on my art to be the best artist I could be. As I love art, this was a joy to me. What do you love to do? Is this your gift.? Is your gift hidden? Maybe you need to unwrap some of your talents to see what God has planned for you. Unwrap it. It's inside of you. Use your gifting for what God has intended. Be you. Be unique. Don't compare yourself to someone else. God created you to be just you. We all bring something to the table to share. Come to Jesus' table. He has much to offer you as you have much to offer Him.

We will now go into an encounter with Jesus. Close your eyes and take a deep breath. Now imagine you are dressed in the biblical clothes of a sack dress and headwear with simple sandals. You approach a low wooden table. Jesus is sitting there waiting for you. Jesus says, "Sit down, my precious child. Thank you for joining me at my table. I have much to discuss with you." Look at the table. What do you see? Jesus has many gifts for you. "My child, I have gifts for you. All you have to do is open your heart and receive. I have a never-ending bottle of refreshing, life-giving water. All you have to do is drink in my goodness, read my Word and I will quench your thirst. I have a plate of healings. Believe for healing. Healing in your mind, body and soul. Healing for loved ones. I offer a peace bowl. Draw on my peace in times of trouble. Be still and know that I am God. I have a large dish of grace for you, a gift of love from God. Share this grace to others. Share my love." Ask Jesus, "What is my gifting? I would like to share my gift for your kingdom glory. Show me your heart about my gift and purpose. How can I use it to its fullest?" Listen to Jesus' heart, paint and create what you feel He is showing you. Write His words and journal your thoughts. Ask a parent about what they see in your painting.

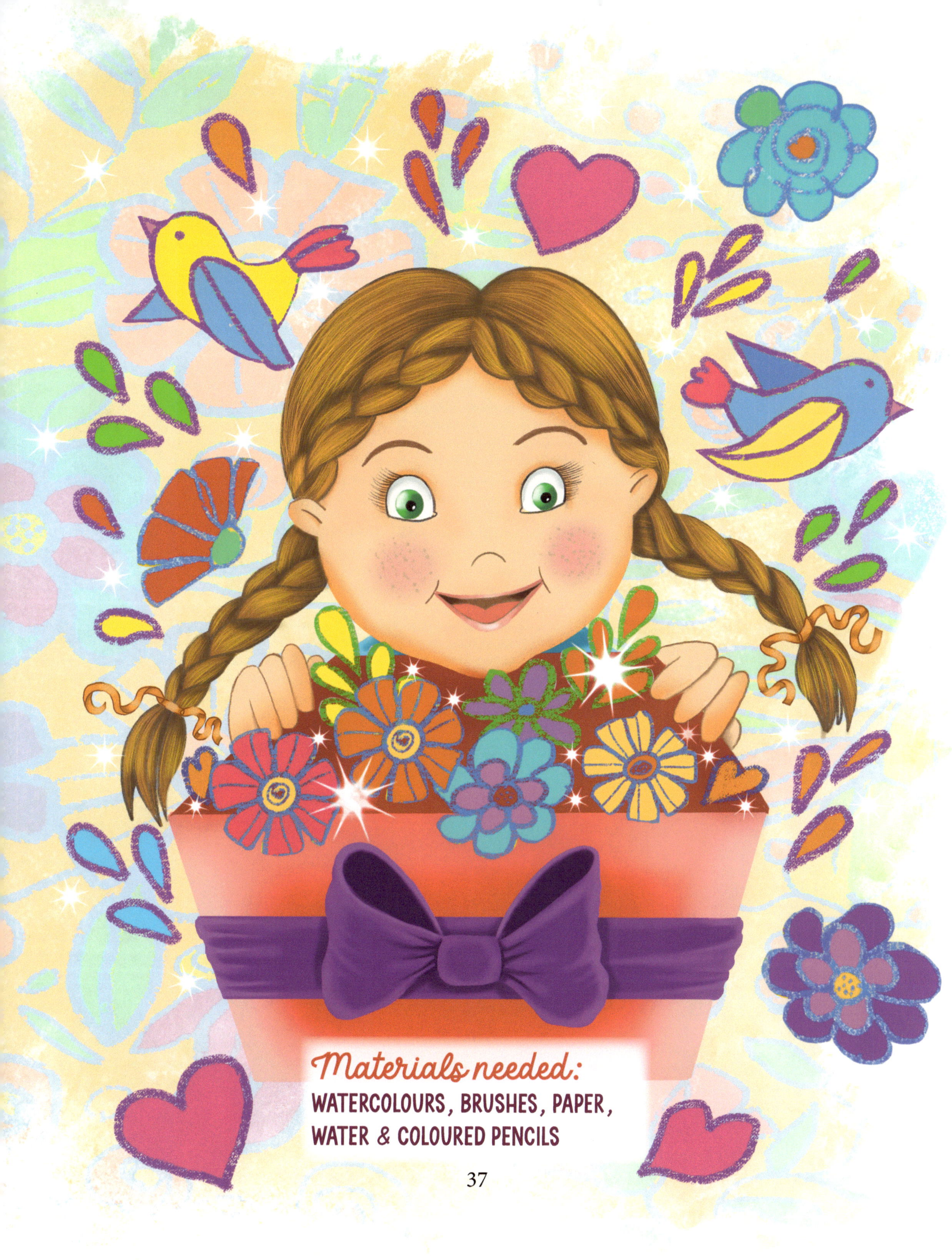

Materials needed:
WATERCOLOURS, BRUSHES, PAPER,
WATER & COLOURED PENCILS

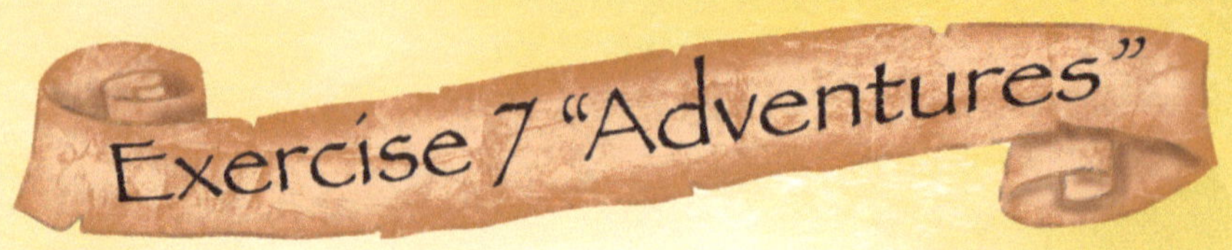


As we have discovered so far with our creations, God can speak to us in the most unusual ways. Sometimes He will show us an object, a colour, a shape, a sign, a song, or a word from someone to show us what is on His heart for us. Have you discovered this in your paintings? In this exercise I encourage you to take a sketchbook and pencil and go outside. Go for a beach walk, a rainforest walk, a walk around your neighbourhood or somewhere completely different. With an adult, of course. And in your quietness ask Jesus to show you something that He wants to bring to your attention. For example, if you are on the beach He might show you a shell that is unusual. Sit down, start to draw this shell and ask Him what He wants to share with you. Another example is, you might be walking through a forest and you see a bird with strange multi-coloured wings. Sketch it and ask Him what He is highlighting about this bird. What is He saying? Question it. Maybe the sun rays are shining down on the bird. Then Jesus might be saying God's glory is shining down on you.

## Ask Jesus to go on an adventure with you.

Use your imagination, have fun and create. Collect shells or other objects and make a collage from your collection. Pray before you create and let God co-create with you to produce a prophetic collage. Maybe it's meant for someone to bless them. Always remember to be still, invite Jesus to be with you, flow with His thoughts (ask questions), create and journal.

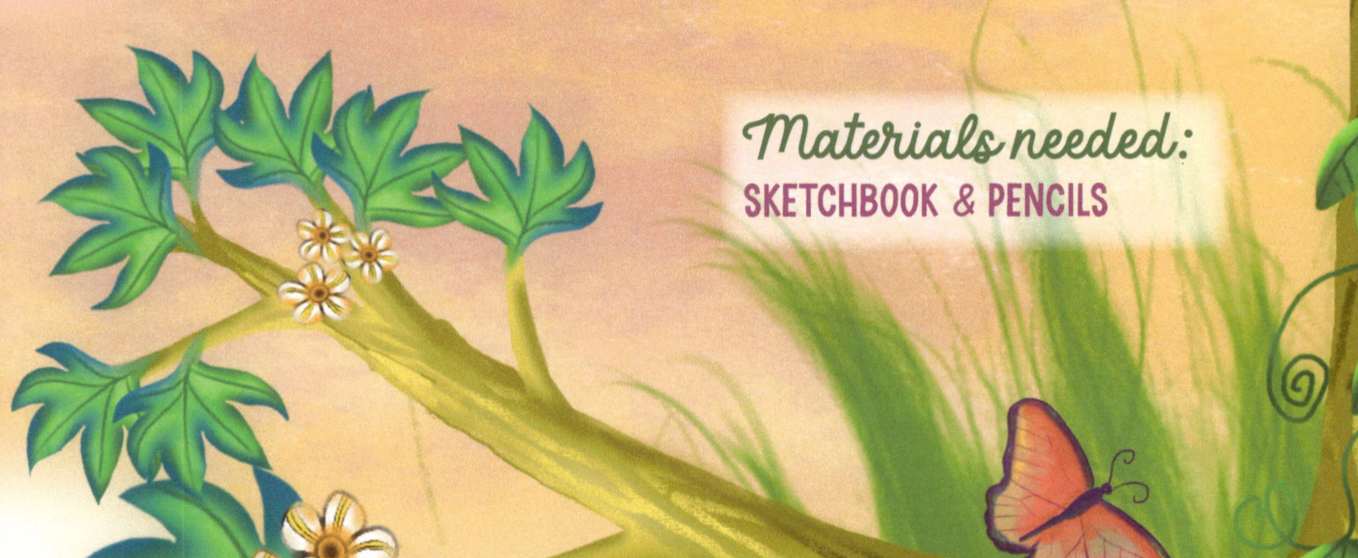

**Materials needed:**
**SKETCHBOOK & PENCILS**

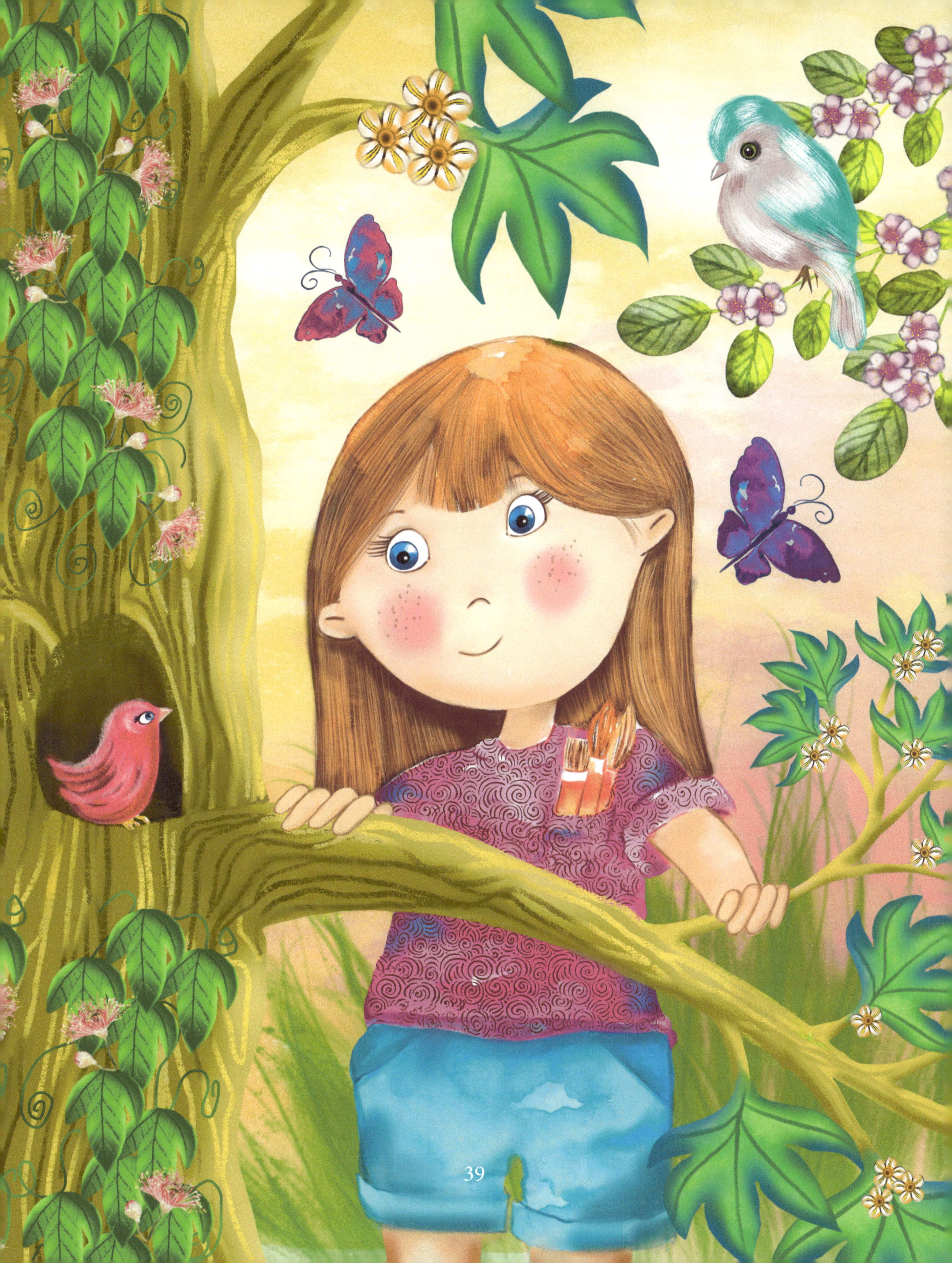

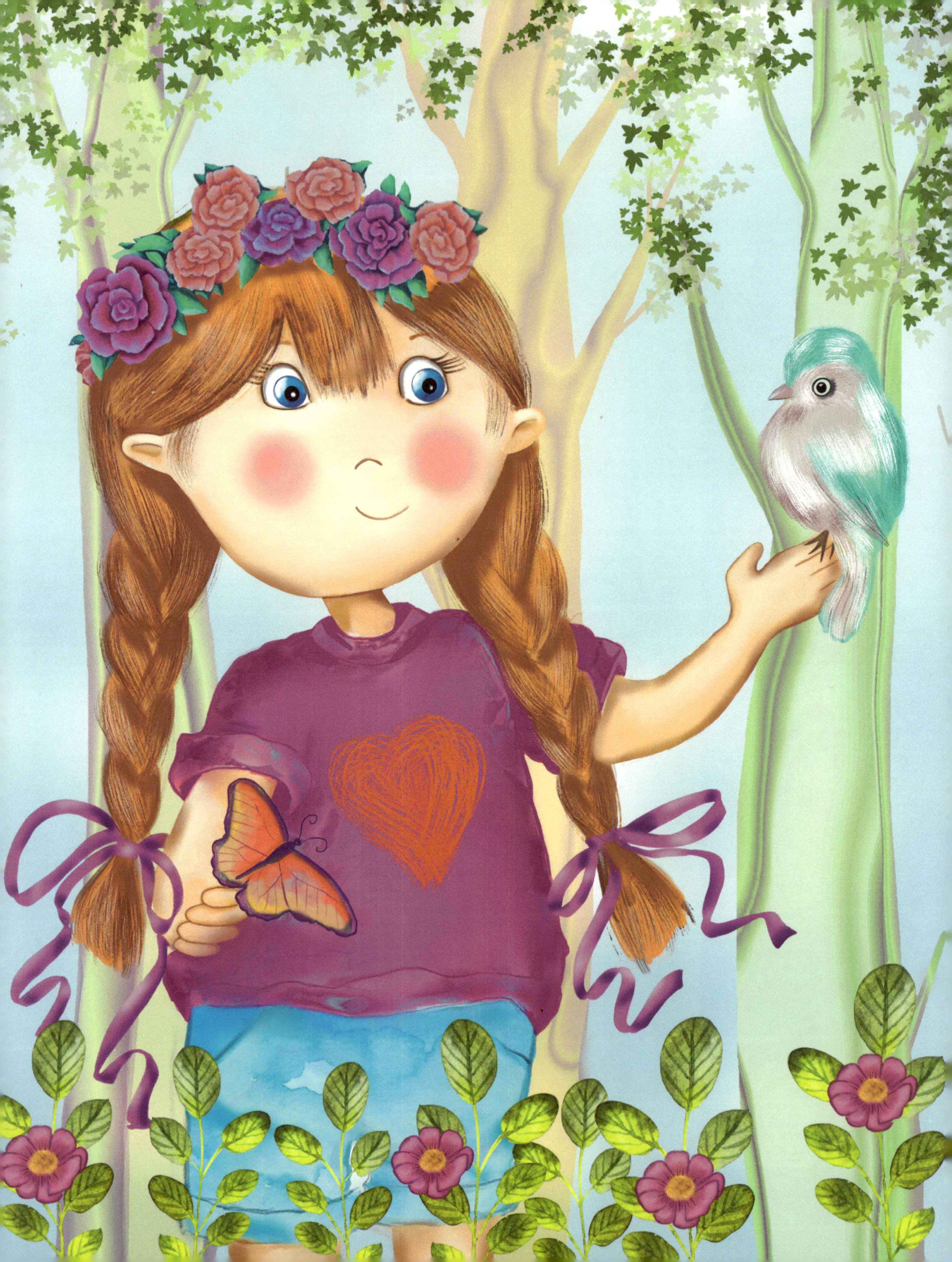

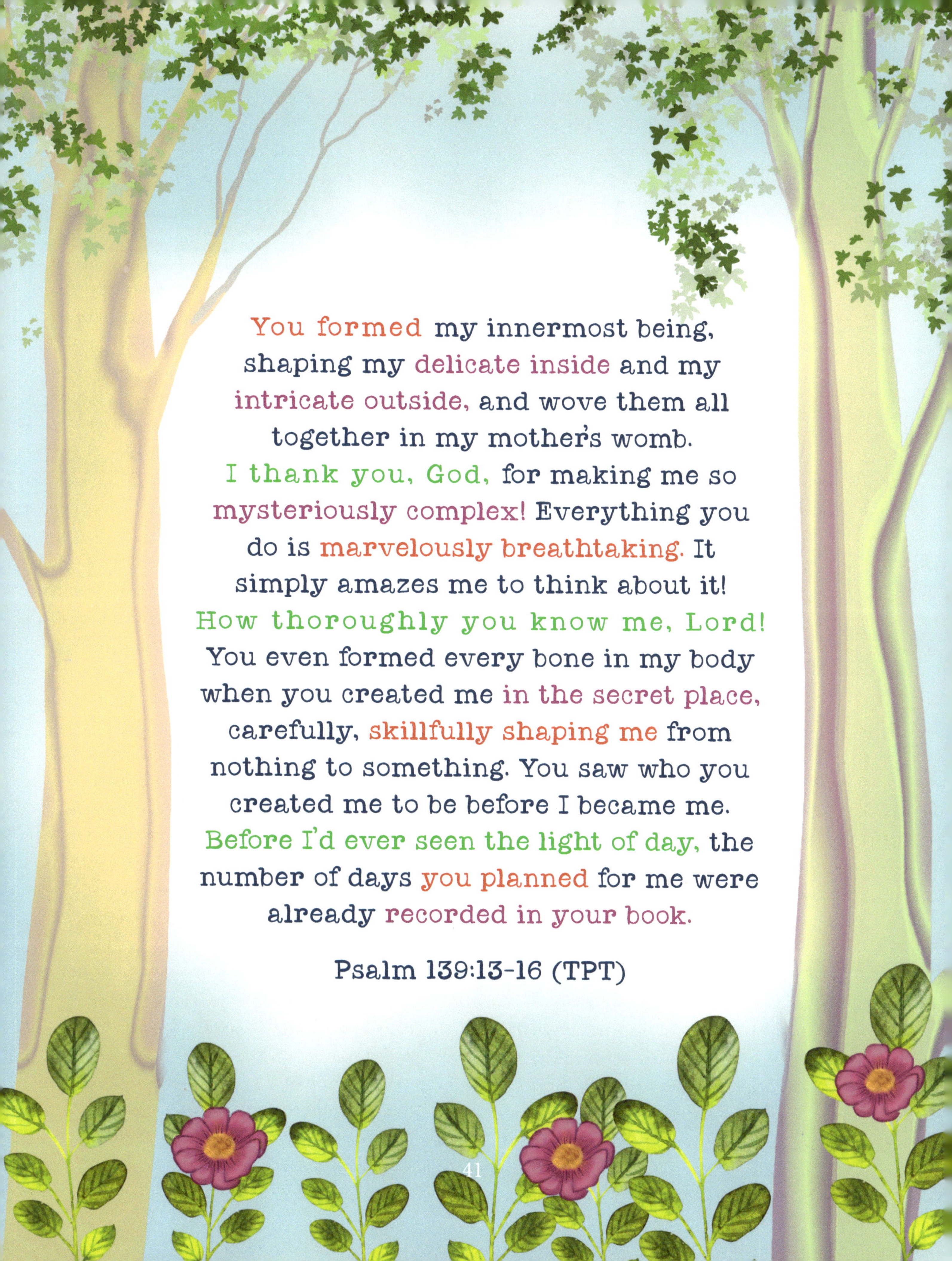

You formed my innermost being, shaping my delicate inside and my intricate outside, and wove them all together in my mother's womb. I thank you, God, for making me so mysteriously complex! Everything you do is marvelously breathtaking. It simply amazes me to think about it! How thoroughly you know me, Lord! You even formed every bone in my body when you created me in the secret place, carefully, skillfully shaping me from nothing to something. You saw who you created me to be before I became me. Before I'd ever seen the light of day, the number of days you planned for me were already recorded in your book.

Psalm 139:13-16 (TPT)

**DO YOU WANT TO HAVE A *relationship* WITH *Jesus* AND HAVE HIM AS YOUR *close friend?* PRAY THIS *simple prayer* AND *invite Him* INTO *your heart.***

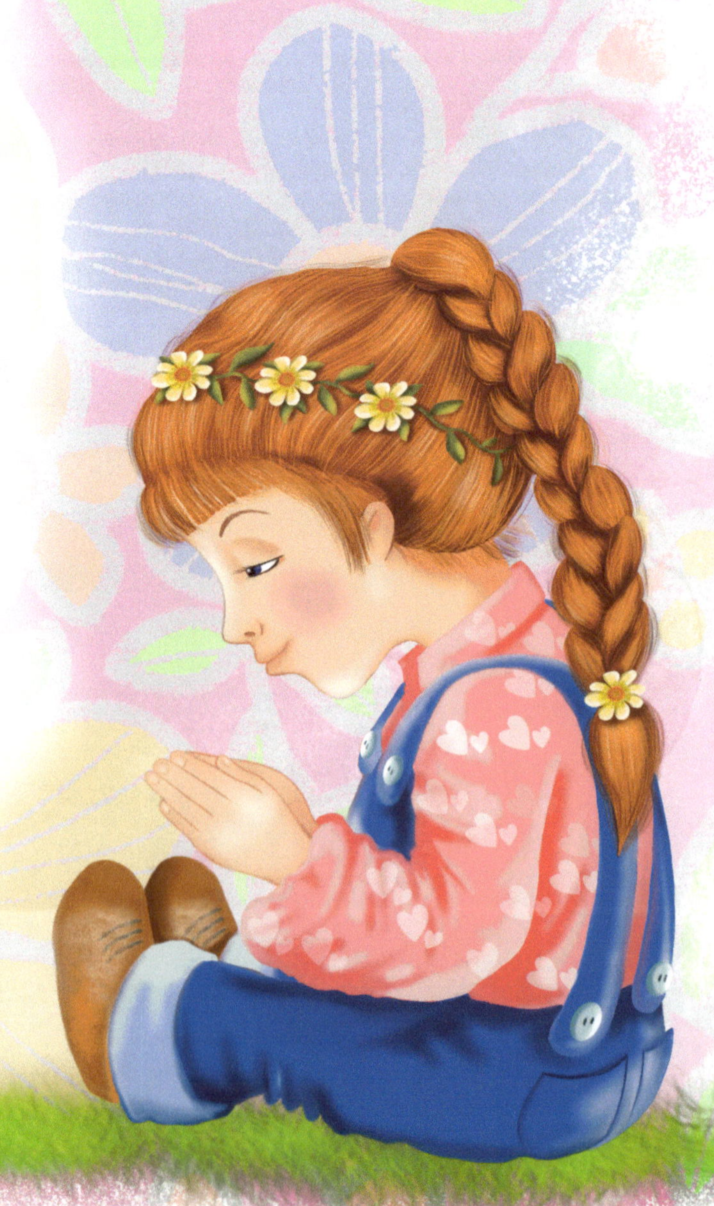

## Dear Jesus,

I know that sometimes I do things I shouldn't and I am sorry. You came to earth and sacrificed your life for me because you love me so much. Thank you for loving me so much that you died for me. Please forgive me of my sin and come into my heart. Help me to do the things you want me to do and to not do wrong. I believe in you. I want to follow you, Jesus.

## Amen.

TRUST IN *the Lord*
WITH ALL YOUR HEART
AND *lean not* ON YOUR
OWN UNDERSTANDING;
IN ALL *all your ways*
SUBMIT TO HIM,
AND *he will*
MAKE YOUR PATHS
*straight.*

**PROVERBS 3:5-6 (NIV)**

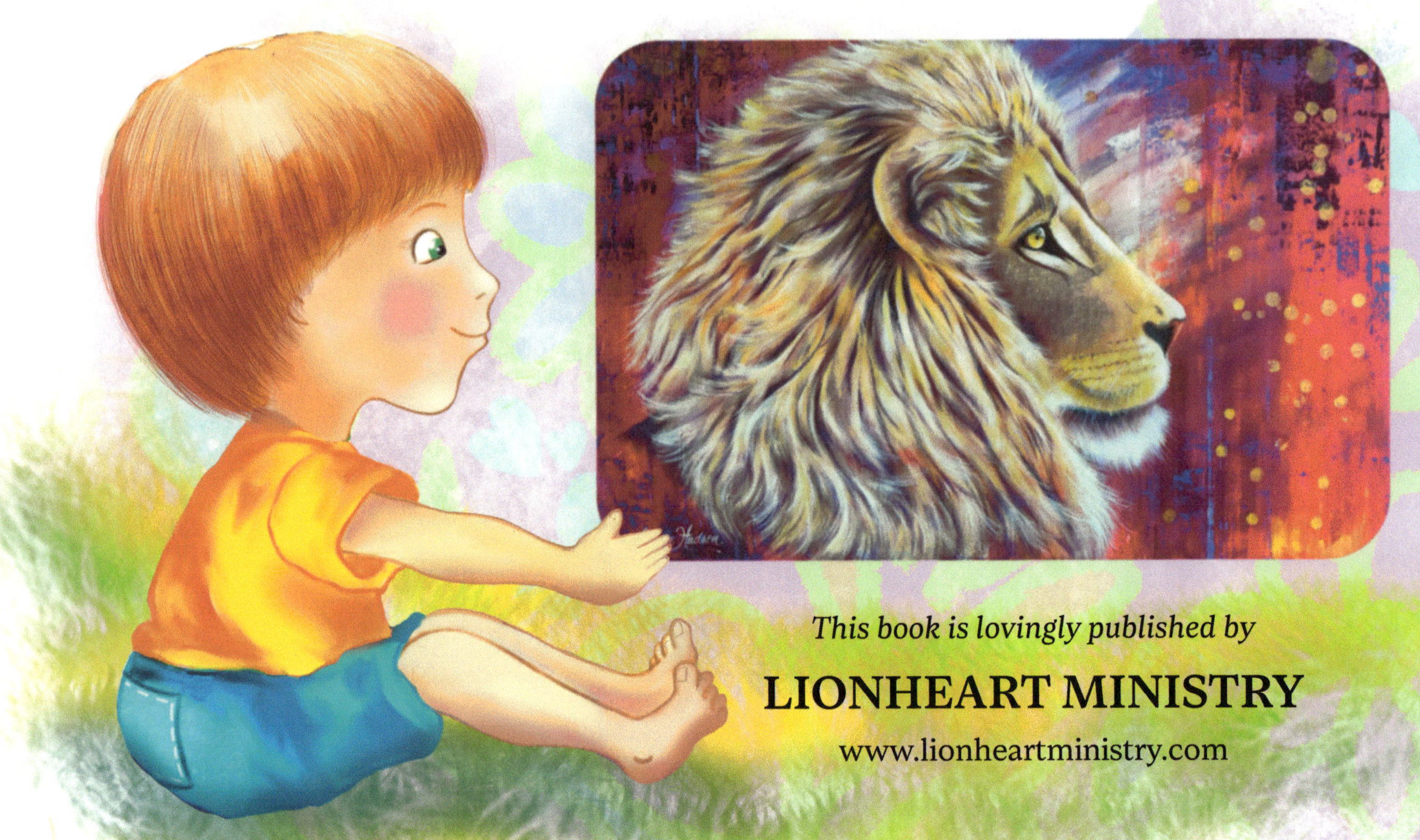


# Thank yous

I would love to sincerely thank the co-founders of Lionheart Ministry, Jonathan and Carrie Christopher. Without their encouragement and generosity this book would not have been published. Thank you for believing in my ministry of prophetic art. Carrie tirelessly pushes women to fulfil their artistic, Godly destinies for the Kingdom. She has an anointed gift of words that birth the heavenly imagination to step into God's presence.

I would also like to thank the talented and gifted Lindsey Sullivan. Lindsey is such a unique gift to me and so many, a talented songwriter and musician, journalist and artist. Her help with the graphic design and editing was invaluable.

I thank my husband John Hudson, for his endless loving encouragement and support, and belief in my giftings.

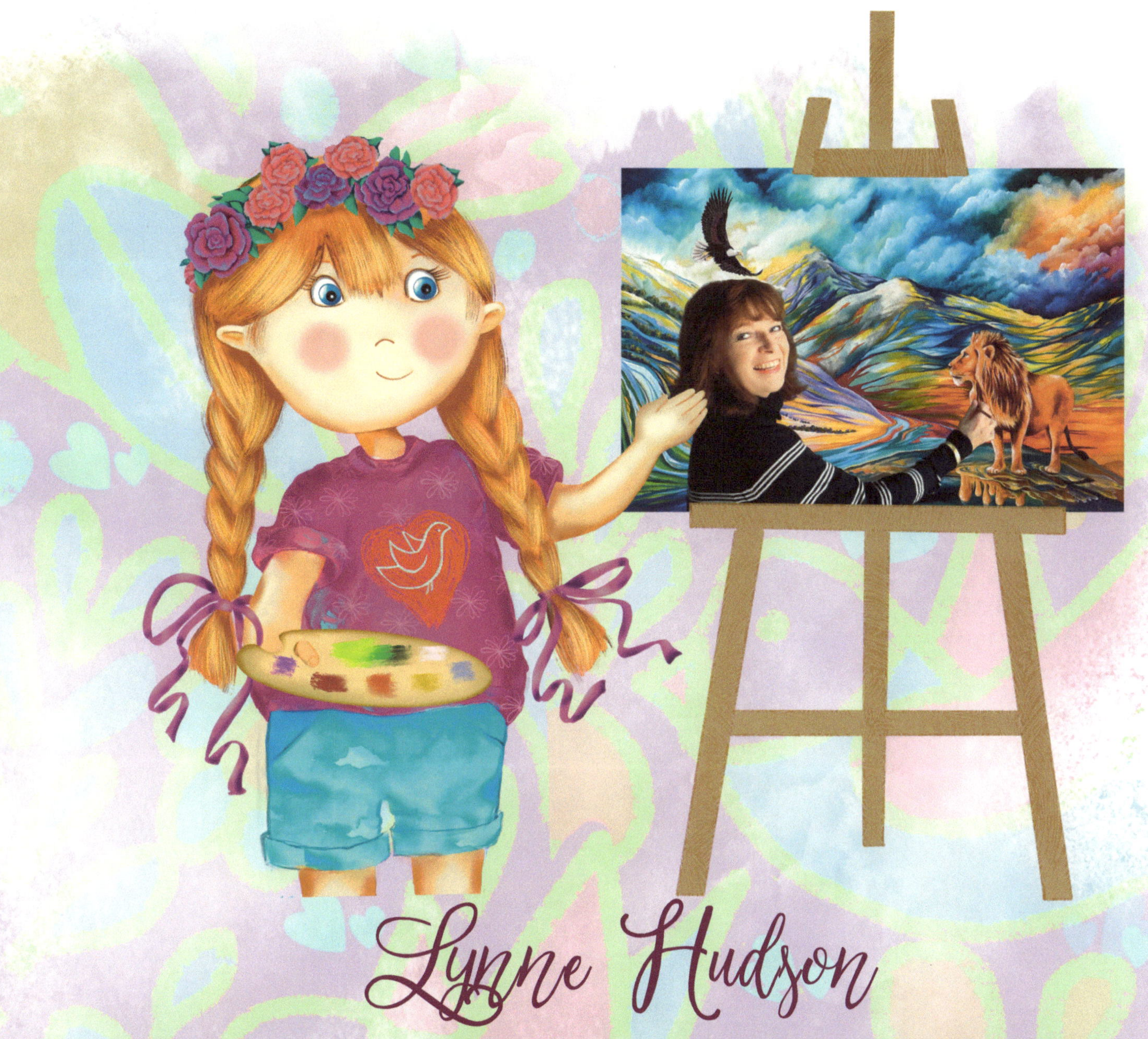

# Lynne Hudson

Lynne has been a professional artist for over forty years. Her work includes creating private painting commissions for clients. She has a special love for illustrating children's books, including Christian books and media. Lynne has been humbled to have held many successful art exhibitions with her works, including exhibitions in Australia and New York City. Her journey has embraced a love and joy of prophetic art, from live painting with worship, to private commissions, to teaching courses on the magnitude of hearing from God through creativity. Lynne paints the promises of God in the prophetic positioning and power of the Lord, radiantly displaying artwork from on high.

Lynne resides on the Gold Coast, Queensland, Australia.

Connect with Lynne at www.lynnehudson.com

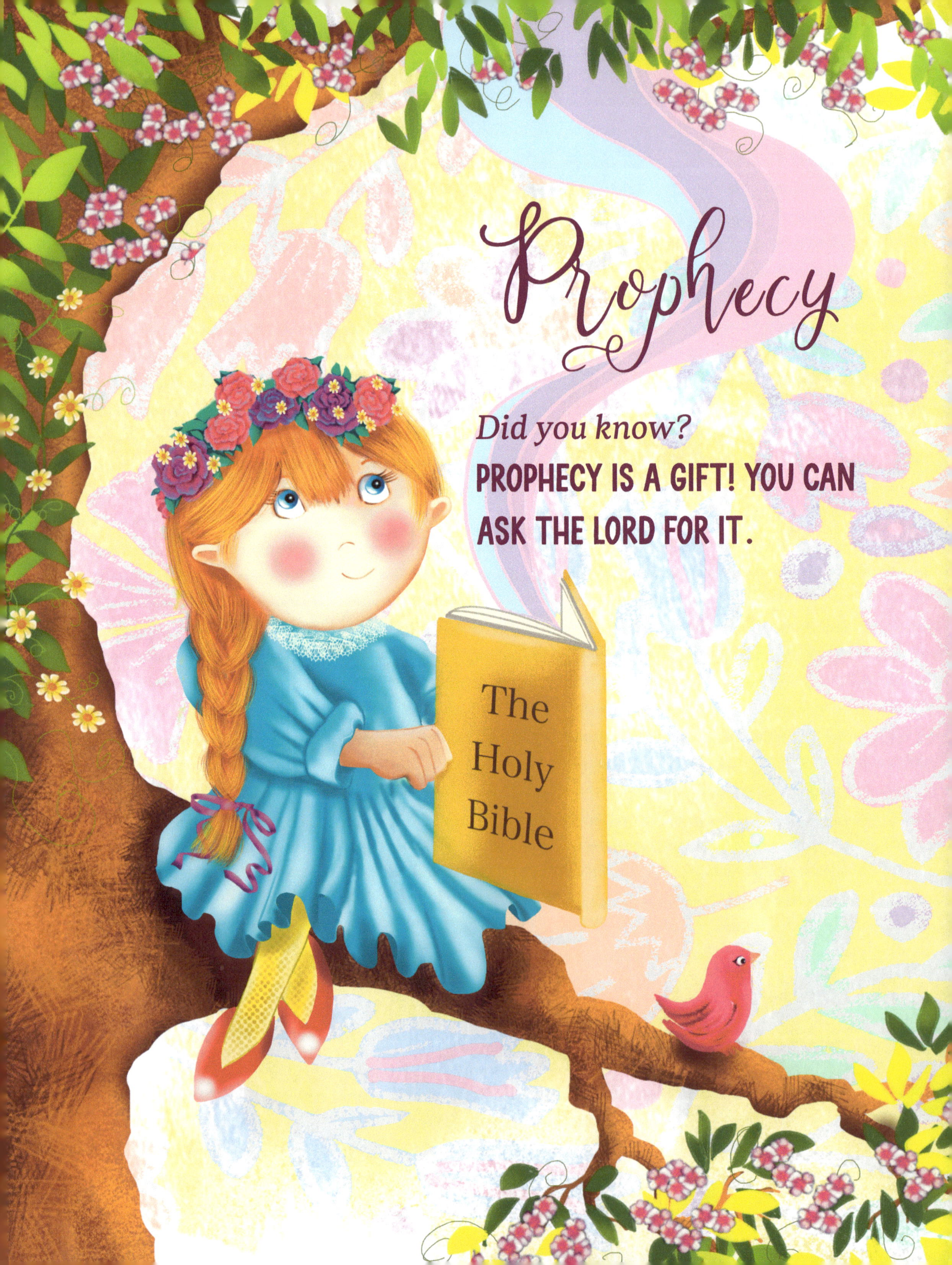


Prophecy

Did you know?
PROPHECY IS A GIFT! YOU CAN
ASK THE LORD FOR IT.

The
Holy
Bible

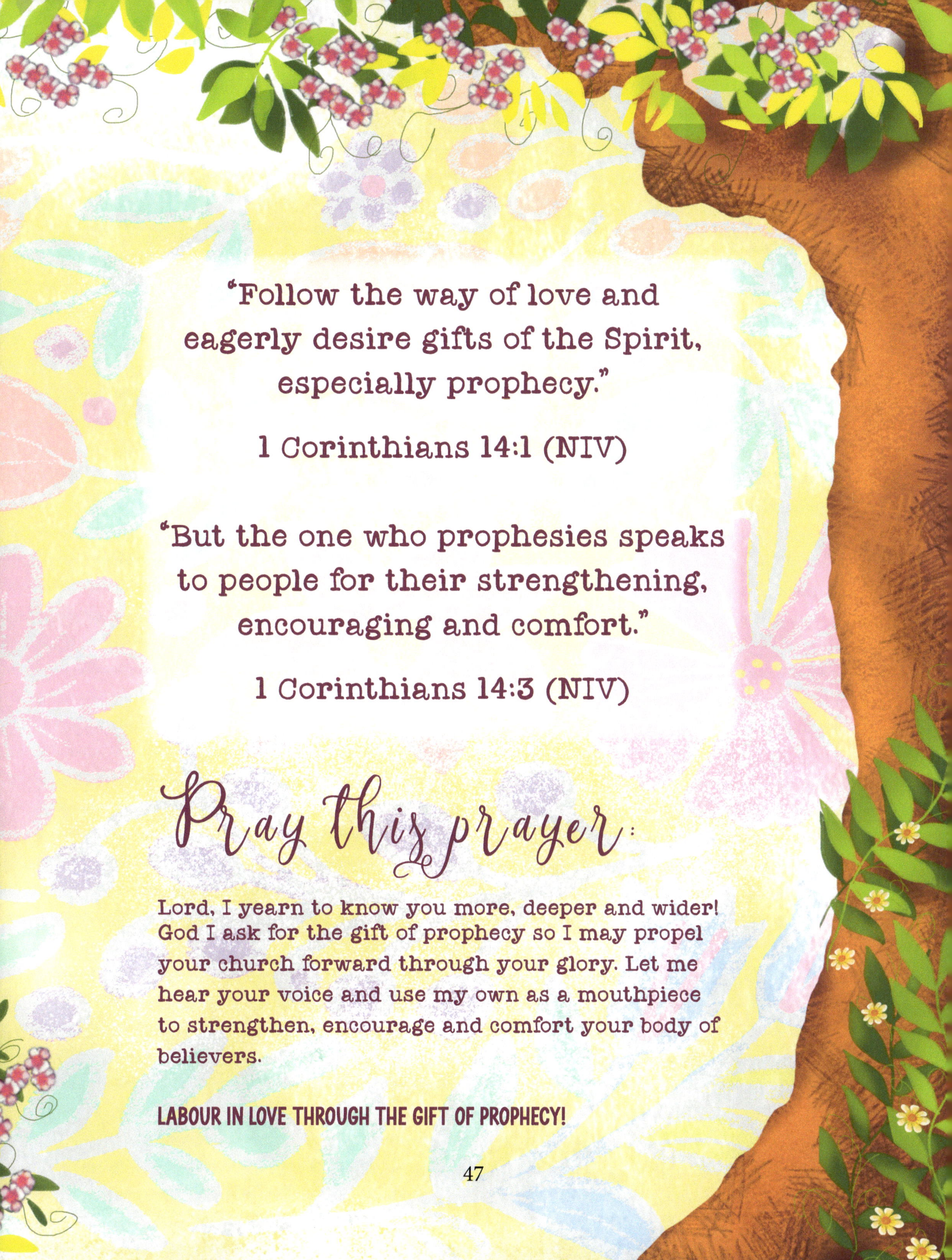

"Follow the way of love and eagerly desire gifts of the Spirit, especially prophecy."

1 Corinthians 14:1 (NIV)

"But the one who prophesies speaks to people for their strengthening, encouraging and comfort."

1 Corinthians 14:3 (NIV)

## Pray this prayer:

Lord, I yearn to know you more, deeper and wider! God I ask for the gift of prophecy so I may propel your church forward through your glory. Let me hear your voice and use my own as a mouthpiece to strengthen, encourage and comfort your body of believers.

**LABOUR IN LOVE THROUGH THE GIFT OF PROPHECY!**

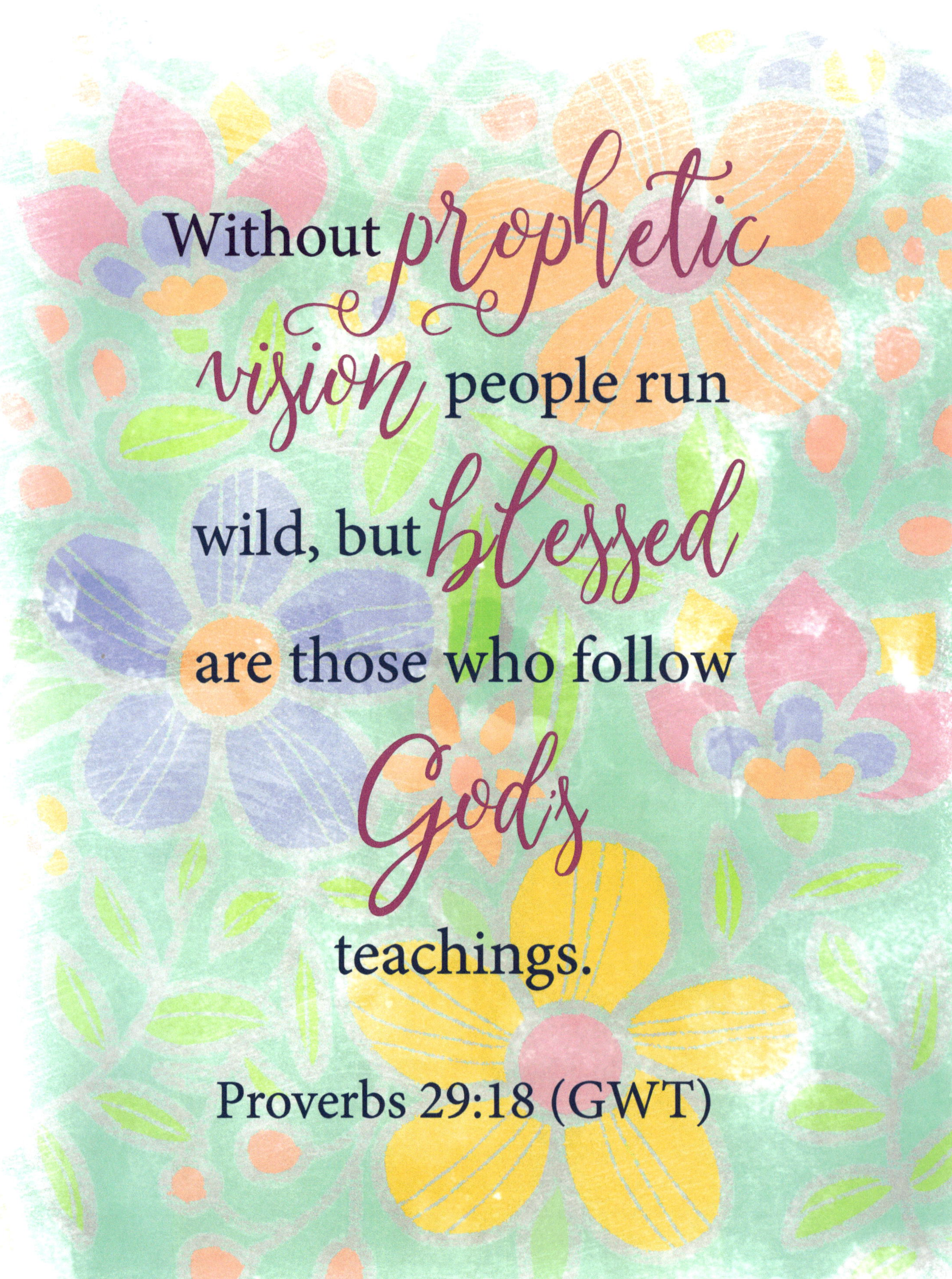

Without prophetic vision people run wild, but blessed are those who follow God's teachings.

Proverbs 29:18 (GWT)